Easy Review ™

for

Federal Income Tax

BY

Amy B. Gitlitz, Esq.

Contributing Editors

Kenneth A. Dursht, Esq.

Randy J. Riley, Esq.

Consulting Editor

Mitchell D. Hollander, Esq.

Law Rules Publishing Corporation
Old Tappan, NJ 07675

800-371-1271

Editorial Staff

Marla Goldstein, Esq.

Jared S. Kalina, Esq.

George Jacobo, Ed.

Printed in U.S.A.

To Brian: The ultimate authority.

Library of Congress

ISBN 1-887426-59-0

Note: This review publication is not meant to replace required texts as a
substitute or otherwise. This publication should not be quoted or cited to. It
is meant only to be used as a reminder of some subject matter and is not a
substitute for a comprehensive understanding of the actual materials which it
references or outlines.

TABLE OF CONTENTS

I. OVERVIEW 1

II. INCOME 3

   A. WHAT IS INCOME 3
      1. In General 3
      2. Gross income defined 3
      3. Forms of Gross Income 4
      4. Meals or lodging 6
      5. Certain Fringe Benefits 8
         a. No Additional Cost Service 9
         b. Qualified Employee Discount 11
         c. Working Condition Fringe 11
         d. De Minimis Fringe 11
         e. Qualified Transportation Fringe 11
         f. Qualified Moving Expenses 12
         g. Group Term Life Insurance 14
         h. Property Transferred for Services 16
   B. LOANS 20
      1. Loans Defined 20
      2. Loans Explained 20
   C. WELFARE, SOCIAL SECURITY & UNEMPLOYMENT COMP. 21
      1. Welfare Payments Received 21
      2. Social Security 21
      3. Unemployment Compensation 22
   D. IMPUTED INCOME 22
      1. Imputed Income Definition 22
      2. Imputed Income Illustration 22
   E. BARTER 23
   F. GIFTS, PRIZES AND AWARDS 23
      1. Gifts and inheritances 23
      2. Prizes and awards 24
      3. Rental value of parsonage 25
   G. CAPITAL APPRECIATION, BASIS RECOVERY & REALIZATION 25
      1. Computation of Basis, Gain or Loss 25
         a. Gains from Dealing in Property 25
         b. Amount of Gain/Loss Realized or Recognized 25
      2. Basis of property--cost 28
      3. Adjustments to basis 29

4.   Basis of property acquired from a decedent
("Step-Up" or "Step-Down")....................................31

5.   Basis of property acquired by gifts & transfers....................32

6.   Loss Limitation Rule....................................32

H. ANNUITIES 33

    1.   Annuities & Certain Proceeds of Endowments 34

        a.   Scope of Annuity Included in GI 34

        b.   Exclusion Ratio....................34

        c.   Adjustments in Investment....................34

I.   DISCHARGE OF INDEBTEDNESS....................35

    1.   Income from discharge of indebtedness....................35

    2.   Part Sale/Part Gift Transaction....................37

    3.   Wagering losses....................38

J.   ILLEGAL INCOME....................39

    1.   Expenditures from Illegal Sale of Drugs....................39

K. INSURANCE PAYMENTS FOR INJURY & SICKNESS....................40

    1.   Compensation for injuries or sickness....................40

    2.   Amounts received under accident & health plans....................42

    3.   Employer Contrib. to Accident & Health plans....................43

L.   TAX EXEMPT INTEREST AND TAX EXPENDITURES....................43

    1.   Interest on state and local bonds 43

    2.   Income from United States savings bonds used to pay higher
education tuition and fees....................44

    3.   Private activity bond and qualified bond 45

    4.   Exempt Facility Bonds....................46

    5.   Mortgage revenue bonds 46

    6.   Qualified Small Issue Bond -- qualified, student
loan bonds, redevelopment bonds....................46

    7.   Qualified 501(c)(3) bond 46

    8.   Volume cap....................46

    9.   Arbitrage bond....................47

    10. Bonds must be registered to be tax exempt 47

    11. Expenses and interest relates to tax exempt income....................47

III. CAPITAL EXPENDITURES....................49

A. CURRENT EXPENSE V. CAPITAL EXPENDITURE 49

    1.   Capital Expenditures....................49

    2.   Certain Expenditures....................51

    3.   Start-up expenditures....................53

B. DEPRECIATION....................54

    1.   Depreciation....................54

    2.   Limitations on Depreciation....................54

    3.   Depreciation Schedule 55

    4. Accelerated cost recovery system (ACRS) 55
        a. Applicable depreciation methods.................................56
        b. Applicable recovery period 57
        c. Applicable convention..57
        d. Classification of Property 58
        e. Double Declining Balance...59
    5. Election to expense certain depreciable assets.....................61
        a. "Recapture" of Depreciation 61
    6. Amortization of goodwill and other intangibles 62

IV. DEDUCTIONS, EXPENSES & LOSSES...................65

A. BUSINESS: LOSSES, EXPENSES AND DEDUCTIONS 66
    1. Trade or Business Expenses...66
    2. Goodwill 71
    3. Expenses for production of income 72
    4. Disallowance of certain expenses: Use of Home, Rental of
       Vacation Homes, Etc 72
    5. Expenditures in connection with the illegal sale of drugs.......75
B. PERSONAL LOSSES 75
    1. Losses..75
        a. Losses Defined..75
        b. Limitations on Losses...76
        c. Loss from wash sales of stock or securities 78
        d. Passive activity losses and credits limited....................78
    2. Personal Expenses..79
        a. Medical, Dental And Other expenses 79
        b. Clothing Expense...80
        c. Legal Fees 81
        d. Education..81
            i. Qualified scholarships 81
            ii. Non-Deductible Educational Costs.......................82
        e. Entertainment...83
            i. Disallowances of certain expenses.......................83
        f. Meals..88
        g. Traveling Expenses..89
        h. Personal, living and family expenses..........................90
            i. In General...90
            ii. Telephone Service 90
            iii. Activities not engaged in for profit 90
            iv. Allowed Deductions...91
            v. Bottom Line..91
    3. Interest..92
        a. Basic Requirements...92

      b.   Limits on Deduction...93
   4. State, Local, Personal & Real Estate Taxes.......................94
   5. Personal Deductions: Donations and Gifts........................95
   6. Tax Consequences of Divorce 98
      a.   Alimony and separate maintenance payments...............98
      b.   Alimony: Allowable Deductions 99
      c.   Alimony: Scope of Limitations 99
      d.   Alimony v. Child Support Payments........................100
      e.   Recapture of Excess Front-Loaded Alimony...............101
      f.   Property Settlements..106

V. TAXABLE INCOME...109

  A. IMPOSITION OF TAX; CALCULATION OF TAXABLE INCOME 109
     1. Calculation of Taxable Income......................................110
     2. Deductions Gets One to AGI 110
         Adjusted gross income defined......................................110
     3. "Above-The-Line" Deductions.......................................110
     4. Taxable income defined...111
     5. "Below-the-line" deductions...112
         Itemized deductions..112
     6. Miscellaneous Itemized Deductions................................113
     7. Overall limitations on itemized deductions 113
     8. Kiddie Tax 115
     9. Maximum capital gains tax rates...................................115
    10. Using Deductions, Exemptions, Dependents and
         the Earned Income Credit 118
      a.   Deductions from GI or Above-the-line......................118
      b.   Distinction: Deduction from GI v. AGI 119
      c.   Personal Exemptions 120
      d.   Dependents..121
      e.   The Tax Credit..122
         i.   Earned income credit 122
         ii. Expenses for household and dependent care necessary
              for gainful employment...................................123

VI. PROPERTY TRANSACTIONS.............................125

  A. CAPITAL ASSETS DEFINED...125
     1. Capital Asset Defined: Revised Statute............................125
     2. Property used in the trade or business & involuntary
         conversions...128
     3. Gain from dispositions of depreciable property.................132
     4. Gain from dispositions of depreciable realty.....................132

	5.	Exchange of property held for productive use or investment . 133	
		Boot	135
	6.	Rollover of gain on sale of principle	139
		EXAMPLES: UNDER IRC § 1034, § 121 AND "THE ACT OF	
		1997	141
	7.	One time exclusion of gain	142
	8.	Involuntary conversions	142
	9.	Certain exchanges of insurance policies	144

VII. CAPITAL GAINS AND LOSSES 145

A.	MAXIMUM TAX RATE ON NET CAPITAL GAIN	145	
	1.	IN GENERAL	146
	2.	CAPITAL GAIN OR ORDINARY INCOME	147
		a. Capital Assets	147
		b. Leasehold Interests	147
	3.	Losses on worthless securities	148
	4.	Determination of gain or loss realized & recognized	148
	5.	Four Exceptions to Gain/Loss Rule	149
B.	CAPITAL GAINS AND LOSSES	149	
	1.	Distinction between long & short-term capital gain	149
	2.	Limitation on capital losses	151
	3.	Capital loss carrybacks and carry-overs	151
	4.	50% Exclusion for gains on small business stock	153
	5.	Summary of The new IRC § 1045	153

VIII. ASSIGNMENT OF INCOME................................155

A.	INTRODUCTION	155	
B.	INCOME DERIVED FROM PERSONAL SERVICES		
	- SPLITTING OF INCOME	156	
C.	INCOME DERIVED FROM PROPERTY	157	
	Real Property In a Community Property State	158	
D.	SERVICES OR INCOME?	158	
E.	PROPERTY HELD IN TRUST	160	
F.	TAXATION OF TRUSTS	160	
	1.	In General	160
	2.	Tax imposed	161
	3.	Distributable net income (DNI)	162
	4.	Special rule for gain on property transferred to trust	
		at less than fair market value	162
	5.	Simple trust	162
	6.	Inclusion of amounts in gross income of beneficiaries	
		of trusts distributing current income	162

7.   Deduction for estates and trusts accumulating income or distributing corpus.......................................163
8.   Inclusion of amounts in gross income of beneficiaries of estates and trusts.......................................163
9.   Throwback Rules 163
10. Charitable Remainder Trust...........................163
11. GRANTOR TRUSTS 163
12. Trust income, deductions, and credits attributable to grantor trusts and others as substantial owners...........................164

G.   DEFINITIONS AND RULES 165
1.   Adverse Person 165
2.   Reversionary interest (Clifford Doctrine)...........................165
3.   Power to control beneficial enjoyment............................165
4.   Administrative powers...................................166
5.   Power to revoke...............................166
6.   Income for benefit of grantor 166
7.   Person other than the grantor treated as substantial owner....166

IX.   BUSINESS ASSOCIATIONS 169

A. PARTNERSHIPS...169
1.   Partners, not partnership, is subject to tax.......................169
2.   Income and credits of partner........................169
3.   Partnership computations..................................169
4.   Partner's distributive share............................170
    a.   Family Partnerships....................................170
    b.   Pass-thru of items to shareholders............................171
B. CORPORATIONS 171
1.   Corporate Taxation Model..............................171
    a.   Double Tax Model....................................171
    b.   Tax Imposed on Corporations....................................171
2. Limitation on use of cash method of accounting.................171
3. Allocation of income and deductions among corporations 172
4. Exemption from tax on corporations 173

X.   METHODS OF ACCOUNTING...........................175

A. IN GENERAL..175
1.   Taxable Year 175
2.   General Rules for Methods of Accounting.......................175
B. METHODS OF ACCOUNTING: IN DETAIL...........................176
1.   CASH METHOD..176
    a.   C Corporation May Not Use Cash Method................176
    b.   Cash Method Illustrated..176
    c.   Cash Method Rules 177

   Economic Benefit Theory..177
   Constructive Receipt..177
  2. ACCRUAL METHOD..179
   All Events Test..179
   Prepaid Subscription Income 180
  3. INSTALLMENT METHOD 180
   Prepaid dues income for certain membership organizations . . 181
   Limitations on deductions for certain..............................183
  4. INVENTORY ACCOUNTING..184
   a. General rules 184
   b. Cost of Goods Sold 184
   c. LIFO 184
   d. FIFO 184

XI. NET OPERATING LOSS, CLAIM OF RIGHT, TAX BENEFITS RULE...187

 A. NET OPERATING LOSS (NOL).......................................187
  1. Net Operating Loss (NOL) Deduction..........................187
  2. CLAIM OF RIGHT 188
   a. Claim of Right: In General 188
   b. Claim of Right: In Detail 190
  3. TAX BENEFIT RULE...190
   a. In General..190
   b. Recovery of tax benefit items 191

XII. DEPLETION 193

 A. DEPLETION: IN GENERAL...193
 B. DEPLETION: IN DETAIL..193
  1. Allowance of deduction for depletion........................193
  2. Basis cost depletion 193
  3. Computation of cost depletion:...............................194
  4. Percentage depletion..194
  5. Depletion Pertaining to Oil, Gas & Minerals Producers.......194
   a. Oil & Gas Producers 194
   b. Economic Interests: Minerals........................195
   c. Intangible Drilling Expenses 195

XIII. TAX SHELTERS...197

 A. TAX SHELTERS: IN GENERAL......................................197
  1. Deferral 197
  2. Conversion 197
 B. TAX SHELTERS: IN DETAIL.......................................197
  1. Classic Tax Shelter..197

    2.   Losses From Investments In Property And The S&L Crisis 198
    3.   Qualified Pensions......................................199
           Qualified Pension, profit sharing and stock bonus plans......199
    4.   INDIVIDUAL RETIREMENT ACCOUNTS (IRAS)..................200
        a.   Individual retirement accounts................................200
        b.   Effect of the 1997 Act...200
        c.   Roth IRA 201
        d.   Education Savings................................201

C. ANTI-TAX SHELTER PROVISIONS 203
    1.   Restriction on investment interest 203
    2.   Capitalization Requirement 203
    3.   Not For Profit Activities 203
    4.   Deduction Limit.......................................203
    5.   Alternative Minimum Tax 204
        a.   AMT: in General 204
        b.   AMT imposed 205
        c.   Adjustments in AMT..206
        d.   Items of tax preference..206
        e.   Denial of certain losses...206

XVI. LITIGATION WITH THE IRS.............................207

A. Legislative Development: 1998 Act.....................................207
    1.   Taxpayer Restructuring & Reform Act: The 1998 Act........207
    2.   Shift of Burden of Proof 207

TABLE OF CASES..209

INDEX...213

TABLE OF STATUTES 225

I.   OVERVIEW

A principal purpose of virtually any tax system - at least in a democracy - is to raise sufficient funds so that government may continue to function and to provide needed services for its citizens. In the United States, both the Executive and Legislative branches have a continuing role in initiating legislation which, when passed, will determine how much revenue is required and, perhaps more importantly, which segments of society are to bear the burden and in what proportions.

Regardless of whether the taxpayer is an individual, trust, partnership or corporation and notwithstanding the complexity of the issues, virtually all tax questions can be grouped into one (or more) of the following categories:

1. What is Income? Is an item or benefit provided to, or on behalf of, the taxpayer included in his/her/its Gross Income? IRC §§ 61, 71, 72, 74, 117, et. seq.

2. Is an Expense paid or incurred by the taxpayer in connection with the conduct of a trade or business of the taxpayer currently deductible? IRC § 162.

3. Is an Expense paid or incurred by the taxpayer in connection with the activity conducted to make a profit currently deductible, even though the activity does not constitute the conduct of a trade or business by the taxpayer? IRC §§ 212, 262.

4. If the taxpayer makes a long-term investment in particular asset to be used, for example, in connection with the Taxpayer's trade or businesses or income-producing activity, may the investment be taken into account currently or only on the termination of the business or income producing activity, as the case may be? IRC §§ 167, 165, 197, 263, 168.

5. Who is properly taxed on income: the person who receives it or the person who generates it or the person who has dominion and control over it? IRC §§ 671-675.

6. When is income taxed and/or deductible? IRC §§ 441; 461.

Although different legislatures can (and often do) arrive at different legislative responses to these question, the questions remain the same. The balance of this Easy Review outline addresses the issues raised by these questions, and is organized around this structure.

II. INCOME

A . What is income?

1. In General

The starting point for determining a taxpayer's liability for income taxes is Gross Income. Where the taxpayer is an individual, the following steps indicate the information required:

STEP 1:   *Determine* Taxpayer's Gross Income.

STEP 2:   *Subtract* Taxpayer's "Above-the-Line" deductions.

STEP 3:   *Determine* Taxpayer's Adjusted Gross Income (*Subtract* Step 2 from Step 1).

STEP 4:   *Subtract* the larger of Taxpayer's
i.   "Itemized" Deductions (IRC § 63); or
ii. "Standard" Deduction (IRC § 63);

Also Subtract the Taxpayer's Personal and/or Dependency Exemptions" (IRC §§ 151 and 152).

STEP 5:   Compute Taxable Income (*Subtract* Step 4 from Step 3).

STEP 6:   Apply tax rates IRC § 1.

STEP 7:   Apply credits to reduce tax liability.

2.   Gross income defined: IRC § 61(a)(1)

Gross Income means "all income" from whatever source derived including (but not limited to) the following items:

a. Compensation for services, including fees, commissions, fringe benefits and similar items; b. Gross income derived from business; c. Gains derived from dealings in property; d. Interest; e. Rents; f. Royalties; g. Dividends; h. Alimony and separate maintenance payments; i. Annuities; j. Income from life insurance and endowment contracts; k. Pensions; l. Income from discharge of indebtedness;

m. Distributive share of partnership gross income; n. Income in respect of a decedent; and o. Income from an interest in an estate or trust.

The Internal Revenue Code does not define "all income," which has been left for case law to develop, but there are guidelines established by the Regulations (Regs.).

Example:

A invests $100 for 100 shares of stock of a corporation traded in the Over-the-Counter market. She holds the stock for many years during which there have been periods when the stock has been valued well in excess of what she paid for it. Of course, the converse has also been true.

However, none of these day-to-day fluctuations in value prior to a sale or exchange of those shares have tax significance, since A did not close out her investment in any of those years. This year, however, A sells the stock for $500. On the sale, A has realized a profit of $400. Absent other facts, this gain will be *recognized*. That is, she will report this gain and pay any resultant tax on her tax return in the year in which her investment was closed out, which is the year in which the sale occurred.

If instead A, rather than selling her stock, had used it as collateral to secure a loan of $500. Then, in that case, there would be no *income* realized by A, since the *cash received* by her would be offset by her *obligation to repay* the loan, with interest.

3. Forms of Gross Income (GI)
* Reg. § 1.61-1 Income may be Realized in any form, not only cash; income can be property, services, stock and meals

* Reg § 1.61-2(d)(1) Income includes the Fair Market Value (FMV) of services or property received as compensation for services.

* Any increase in *net worth* is presumed income unless specifically excluded within the code.

* A taxable event (i.e., *realization*) is necessary before any incremental increases of decreases in the value of property held by a taxpayer can have significance for tax purposes.

* Exclusions from GI must be specified within the Code.

Glenshaw Glass, Co. v. Comm'r., 348 U.S. 426 (1955).
Taxpayer, a plaintiff in an antitrust action, sought compensatory
damages and punitive damages relating to defendant's alleged violation of
antitrust laws. Taxpayer recovered: (i) compensatory damages, measured
by profits lost due to defendant's actions; and (ii) punitive damages.
While it conceded that the compensatory damages were taxable, it argued
that the punitive damages were not "earned" and, in fact, were a mere
(non-taxable) "windfall".
Held: Punitive damages, no less than the compensatory damages, were
"clearly realized" accessions to taxpayer's wealth.

This statement regarding damages has become *de facto* the functional
definition of income for purposes of the Internal Revenue Code. To be
included in a taxpayer's gross income, there must be an accession to
"wealth" (a bonafide loan is not taxable due to the taxpayer's real
obligation to repay) and the accession must be "clearly realized."
Realization ordinarily occurs when the income becomes subject to the
taxpayer's dominion and control. Finally, the item must not otherwise
be "excluded" or subject to specific treatment elsewhere in the Code.
See, e.g., Capital Gains, IRC § 1201 et. seq.; "Nonrecognition"
exchanges, IRC §§ 1031, 1033; and Reg § 1.61-14(a), *infra*.
The *Glenshaw Glass* case helped develop the basic concept of gross
income:

     i.   An item that represents an *undeniable accession to wealth;*
     ii. that is *clearly realized*; and
     iii. over which the taxpayer has complete *dominion or control*.

Old Colony Trust Co. v. Comm'r, 279 U.S. 716 (1929).
There are many important areas in the tax law that involve this decision.
The Old Colony Trust case establishes that where employer discharges
an obligation for employee, it is nonetheless part of the employee's
gross income. The mere fact that the employer paid the employee's
creditor (here, the Internal Revenue Service) rather than the employee
does not prevent the payment from being treated as compensation
income. Moreover, the compensation is "realized" by the taxpayer -
employee, even though it was never physically delivered to him. The
discharge of employee's obligation is equivalent to receipt and
subsequent repayment of the debt by the employee.

However, not all payments made by an employer to, or on behalf of, an
employee result in income to the employee.

U.S. v. Gotcher, 401 F.2d 118 (5th Cir. 1968).
Mr. and Mrs. Gotcher traveled overseas on an all expense-paid trip provided by Volkswagen. Volkswagen wanted to entice Mr. Gotcher to become a dealer in the U.S. Mr. Gotcher had no control over how the money was spent and any personal benefit of the trip to him was only incidental to the dominant business purpose of the trip. Mrs. Gotcher had to record the trip as GI because she had no business relationship with Volkswagen.

The issue of whether employer payment on behalf of employee (or employee, spouse or companion) in connection with travel income to the employee is a question of intent. If the travel is business-related, the employer payment will likely be excluded (and employer may be able to deduct business expense under § 162). However, if the primary purpose of the trip is to benefit the employee personally, the employer reimbursement will be taxable to the employee. (Again, the employer should be able to deduct this as non-cash compensation paid to the employee). As to amounts paid by the employer which are attributable to the spouse, no deduction is allowed unless the spouse is an employee and the purpose of the trip is business. *See* IRC § 274(m).

4. Meals or lodging furnished for the employer's convenience:
    IRC § 119.

IRC § 119(a) Value of meals or lodging furnished by or on behalf of an employer to an employee, spouse, or dependent *for the convenience of the employer* is excluded from GI. If:

    i.   Meals are furnished *on the business premises of employer*, for the convenience of the employer and with respect to lodging, OR

    ii. Employee is required to accept lodging on the premises *as a condition of employment.*

IRC § 119(b)

    i.   The terms of an employment contract are not determinative of the issue of whether meals were furnished *for the convenience of the employer*; i.e., for a substantial non-compensatory reason.

    ii. The fact that a charge is made, or fact that employee may accept or decline such meals is not to be taken into account.

    iii. If employee is required to pay a fixed charge for meals which are furnished for the convenience of the employer, the employee can exclude such amount from gross income, whether the employee makes the payment or it is taken out of salary.

IRC § 119(c). Camps

Where an employee is furnished lodging in a camp located in a foreign country by or on behalf of her employer, the camp is considered part of the "business premises" of the employer. IRC § 119(c). A camp for this purpose includes: i. lodging furnished in a remote area without satisfactory open housing; ii. which is located as near as practical to the vicinity where individual employee renders services; iii. and which is furnished in a common area, that is one not available to the public; and iv. which normally houses 10 or more employees. IRC § 119(c)(2)(C).

IRC § 119(d). The value of lodging to an employee by educational institutions is excluded from GI if the lodging is located on or near the institution. However, the value is excluded only to the extent that the average rent paid by "outsiders" (i.e., those who are neither students nor faculty of the educational institution) does not exceed the amount paid for comparable lodging or, if less, 5% of the appraised value of the lodging paid by the employee. (IRC § 119(d)(2)). If the school rents such lodging to persons other than faculty or students at a rent lower than 5% of the rental value then the average rental value is substituted.

See IRC § 107, which excludes the rental value of a "parsonage" for a "minister of the gospel."

Note:

In order to exclude the value of lodging furnished to an employee, the noncompensatory nature of the payment must be established in addition to the fact that the lodging so furnished constituted a "business premises" of the employer. It is probably adequate if the taxpayer establishes by credible evidence that substantial duties of his job were performed at the location of the lodging. This may be sufficient to convert the "personal" lodging into "business premises."

Benaglia v. Comm'r, 36 B.T.A. 838 (1937)
Resort manager receives meals and lodging in addition to salary.
Held: Not taxable because meals and lodging were given for the employer's convenience, i.e., a substantial noncompensatory reason to enable the employee to perform the duties of his job as a resort manager.

Practical Application:

As with all compensation-related issues, the intent of the parties controls. The key fact to establish is that the meals and/or lodging were furnished to enable the employee to perform his/her job, rather than to compensate the employee for services being rendered.

For example, with respect to lodging, it is not necessary to prove that the lodging was indispensable to the performance of the duties, only that it was furnished to enable the employee to perform the duties of his job. *See Caratan v. Comm'r.*, F.2d (9th Cir.).

* Convenience is established if employee is on call 24 hours a day (Rev. Rul. 71-411,1971-2 C.B. 103).
* If facilities are more than 60 miles away than convenience is established. (*Setal v. Comm'r.*, 20 T.C.M. 780 (1961)).
* Cash reimbursements are not excluded (under § 119(a)(1)) meals and lodging must be furnished in kind and not cash (*Comm'r. v. Kowalski,* Rev. Rul. 71-411 1971-c.b.
* If choice is restricted because the employee is on call, then it is deductible non-compensatory (*Christy v. U.S.,* 437 F.2d (9th Cir. 1971)).
* Groceries supplied to an individual who lives on the premises are meals within IRC § 119 (*Jacob v. U.S.,* 493 F.2d 1294 (3d Cir. 1974))
* House across or next door to company is "on premises" (*Lindeman v. Comm'r.,* 60 T.C. 609 (1973)), because employee performed "substantial duties" of his position there. *Contra Comm'r. v. Anderson,* 371 F.2d 59 (6th Cir. 1966)), where the taxpayer, a motel manager, lived two short blocks away from the motel. The living premises was not the business premises because the taxpayer did not perform "substantial duties of his job" there.

5. Certain Fringe Benefits: **IRC § 132.**

IRC § 132(a) identifies the following six categories of nontaxable benefits which may be provided to "employees":

    a.   No-additional-cost service (IRC § 132(a)(1))
    b.   Qualified employee discount (IRC § 132(a)(2))
    c.   Working condition fringe (IRC § 132(a)(3))
    d.   De minimis fringe (IRC § 132(a)(4))
    e.   Qualified transportation fringe (IRC § 132(a)(5))
    f.   Qualified moving expense fringe (IRC § 132(a)(6))

Obstacles that may be encountered include:

i.   No additional cost services and qualified discounts must be provided on a non-discriminatory basis; if a different rate is allowed for those receiving higher compensation (the "highly compensated employee") only those in the lower class of compensation are allowed to completely exclude the benefit. (IRC 132(j)(1)).

ii. Employees who wish to exclude benefits attributable to no additional cost services and qualified employee discounts must establish that the items or services furnished rise out of the *line of business in which the employee is engaged in rendering services for the employer.*

iii. The beneficiary of the employer-provided benefits must be an "employee." For this purpose, the term employee is broadly defined - for purposes of qualified employee discounts and no additional cost services only-to include current, retired and disabled employees and the surviving spouse and dependent children of a deceased employee.

iv. The limitations of IRC § 132 apply only top "common law" employee benefits. This section is inapplicable to benefits expressly provided by a statute (IRC § 132(l)).

a. No Additional Cost Service:

According to the legislative committee reports, the "fringe" involves the concept of "excess" capacity. This concept can readily be seen with a scheduled commercial flight on a plane that seats 200 passengers. The plane is scheduled to take off with only 50 passengers booked and on board. An airline employee can use an empty seat on a "stand-by" or "space available" basis provided the benefit is not weighted towards "highly compensated employees."

IRC § 132(b)(1) *"no additional cost service"* service is not included in GI if:

i.   The service is provided by an employer to a regularly employed employee in the ordinary course of the employer's line of business (same as routinely offered to customers) e.g. allow a telephone company employee to make free calls; and

ii. There must be "no additional cost" to employer in providing the benefit. The employer incurs *no additional expense* or cost such as *forgone revenue,* in providing such a service.

Example 1:
Employee works for a hotel chain. While traveling on vacation, he stays at a hotel in his employers organization at a substantially reduced rate. There are plenty of empty hotel rooms. The benefit, whether in the form of discount or a complementary room, should be fully excluded from the employee's gross income. This is exactly the "extra capacity" notion for which the statute was written.

Example 2:
The facts are the same as in the preceding example, except the hotel is full and to accommodate the employee, the hotel must bounce a paying guest. "Bumping a paying guest" involves forgone revenue and, therefore, a substantial additional cost to the employer in providing the service. Thus, the value of the hotel room is not excluded from the Gross Income of the employee.

Example 3:
American Airlines employee is allowed to fly for free on a "space available" basis on her days off.

Analysis:
Qualifies as no additional cost service. Aircraft is taking off with or without the employee.

IRC § 61: benefit to taxpayer therefore include, but
IRC § 132(b): any service provided by employer to employee if:
    i. service is offered for sale to customers in the ordinary course of the line of business in which the employee is performing services, and
    ii. the employer incurs no additional cost in providing the service. Thus, the air fare is excluded from employees Gross Income.

Example 4:
Same facts as Example 3 except that the American Airlines employee is permitted to use hotel owned and operated by American Airlines, but might qualify for an employee discount, which would provide at least a partial tax benefit.

Easy Review for Federal Income Tax

Analysis:
In all probability this would not qualify due to the line of business limitation in IRC § 132(1).

b.   *Qualified employee discount* is not included in GI.
     IRC § 132(c).
A major limitation to the availability of the qualified employee discount is that the property or services provided must also be "qualified" see IRC § 132(c)(4), which states that all property, "other than real property and . . . personal property of a kind held for investment . . . " qualify.

The qualified employee discount "fringe" allows an employee to purchase goods or services routinely sold by the employer at a price at least equal to cost (in the case of goods) or no more than a 20% discount (for services). Only allowed for the goods sold or services within the employers line of business in which the employee performs services that are available to non-employee customers. The form of the qualified discount provided can be price reduction or cash rebate.

For example, if a highly compensated employee receives a 35% discount and a non-highly compensated employee only a 20% discount, the entire discount provided to the highly compensated employee is taxable and not just the additional 15% offered on top to which the highly compensated employee is entitled.

c.   *Working condition fringe* (not included in GI) is property or services provided to an employee: IRC § 132(d). Under such circumstances that had employee paid for the property or services directly, the employee would have been entitled to a deductible business expense (IRC § 162) or depreciable (IRC § 167).
*   Example: use of company car for business purposes or a business publication subscription

d.   *De minimis fringe* (not included in GI) is too small to account for: **IRC § 132(e)** It is treated as administratively impracticable, therefore, the value is excluded from income.
*   Example: personal photocopies, pens, water cooler usage.

Although not likely to be *de minimus*, IRC §132(e)(2) also authorizes the exclusion of a subsidized eating facility provided to an employee by an employer provided the employer at least charges its costs to the employee and the eating facility is located "on or near" the business premises of the employer (contrast IRC § 119) which requires that meals be furnished **on** the business premises of the employer to be excluded.

    e.   *Qualified transportation fringe* (not included in GI) is transportation in a commuter highway vehicle (van with more than 6 people) transit pass ($60 per month) or qualified parking "on or near the business premises of the employer" ($155 limit per month) (adjusted for inflation): **IRC § 132(f)**. This fringe includes an employer provided van pool.

Note: This fringe has specific limitations. Thus, the employer cannot offer to pay $155 a month to an employee towards his commuting expenses. Cash in this instance would be taxable as compensation income to the employee. However, cash may be permissible as a reimbursement for the type of benefit specified.

    f.   *Qualified moving expenses* (not included in GI): **IRC § 132(g)** includes, *inter alia,* cash reimbursements to the extent that the employee would have been entitled to a moving deduction had she paid the cost herself. (IRC § 217).

Example 1:
Ted graduated from Harvard College 2 years ago after majoring in applied mathematics. A software manufacturer in Silicon Valley, California has made him an attractive offer, which includes the cost of moving his personal effects from Washington, D.C. to Los Gatos, California, where the company is located. Since the cost of moving household goods and personal effects and Ted's travel expenses are within the scope of the term "moving expenses" in IRC § 217(b), the benefit provided by the company to Ted is fully excluded as qualified moving expenses under IRC § 132(g).

If, on arrival in California, suitable lodging is somehow unavailable and the company rents one or more rooms for Ted near its business premises, IRC § 132(g) no longer applies. However, depending on the circumstances, Ted might exclude the benefit derived from the hotel rooms either under IRC § 119 lodging provided on the business premises of the employer for a substantial noncompensatory reason (or as a working condition fringe benefit) provided the dominant character of the lodging is to enable Ted to properly perform his job in California.

Analysis:
IRC § 61(a)(1): Value of employer-provided "fringe" is presumptively included in employee's gross income.

IRC § 119(a)(1): Value may, however, be excluded if meal is furnished on business premises for a substantial noncompensatory reason. Here, the problem seems to be whether the neighborhood restaurant constitutes a business premises of the employer. If done on a sporadic, infrequent basis, argument may be persuasive. However, where this is an every night affair, IRC § 119 won't apply. *See Moss v. Comm'r., infra.*

Example 2:
American Airlines runs a chain of health clubs, which they allow the pilots to use.

Analysis:
Fails line of business test under IRC § 132(b)(1). Health club is not in pilots' line of business.

Example 3:
An employee of a soft drink "conglomerate" is employed in the accounting department of the soft drink "business." He uses the company plane to fly to company owned resort in the Bahamas which he uses for a week. Those benefits are includible, since the line of business in which he is employed does not involve the airline or the hotel.

In contrast, if he were employed in a position, such as a vice-president or general counsel, which affected all of the lines of business of the conglomerate, the value of the fringe benefits would be excluded.

Example 4:
Joan works at Neiman Marcus and gets a 30% discount on a $100 dress, for which she paid $70. ($100 - 30 = $70).
Is the $30 income?
One could argue *Gotcher* in that this primarily benefits Neiman's. But what if Joan purchases a bathing suit which she does not wear in the store?

Analysis:

IRC § 132 (a)(2):   Qualified employee discount:

IRC § 132 (c)(3):   Employee discount defined: the amount of the price to employee is less than price to customers.

IRC § 132 (c)(4):   qualified property or services: offered for sale to customers in the ordinary course of business in which the employee is performing services.

Limitations: IRC § 132 (c)(1)(A)+(B): (A) property: the gross profit percentage (GPP) of price at which the property is being offered by employee to customers.

Thus: Employee discount (30%) b=$30
GPP of Neiman Marcus = Usual Profit (mark-up) =
Aggregated price sold of $20mm/yr. (less cost of
goods sold $5 mm/yr.)= $15mm or 75% GPP
Price to customers = $100
Is employee discount less than or equal to GP? If "yes," Discount is excessive.

Price to Customers
100 - 70 is less than 75% G.P.
30 less than or equal to 75
(excluded from GI under IRC § 132 (a)(2))

g.   Group term life insurance purchased for employees: IRC § 79

  i.   Tax Free Limits on Group Term Life

IRC § 79(a) Permits an employer to provide up to $50,000 of group term life insurance coverage without adverse tax consequences. Where coverage exceeds $50,000, the excess cost is taxed to the employee, but at very attractive rates. *See* IRC 79(c); Reg § 1.79-1.

Group Term Life Insurance is not included in GI if:
*   Employer is beneficiary indirectly or directly.
*   Person described in IRC § 170(c) (Charity) is the sole beneficiary.

* Insurance must be supplied on a non-discriminatory basis. IRC § 79(d)
* Can't discriminate as to who or in what amount.
* Can't favor key employees, as defined by IRC § 416(i), for eligibility.
* Insurance must benefit 70% or more of all employees.
* At least 85% of all participants in the plan must be other than key employees.

ii. Permissible Exclusions: IRC § 79(d)(3)(b)

* Employees who have not completed at least three years of service.
* Part-time or seasonal employees.
* Employees who are not part of the plan but are part of a special union or collective bargaining agreement that negotiated the benefits.
* Non-resident alien employees who have no earned income from U.S. sources (see IRC §§ 911(d)(2); 861(a)(3)).

iii. Certain death benefits: IRC § 101

The proceeds of life insurance contracts are excluded from GI as long as such amounts are paid "by reason of the death of the insured." Exclusion for benefits are applicable upon death of the insured, unless the Life Insurance contract is cashed in or the policy is sold prior to death.

iv. Sale/Transfer of Value: IRC § 101

IRC § 101(a)(2) If there is a sale or other "transfer for value," of the policy for valuable consideration, the exclusion is limited to the total of the amount of consideration paid (actual value) by the transfer and the subsequent premiums paid by the transferee after the transfer.

Example:
A assigns a policy on A's life to T, in exchange for a consideration. Upon A's death, T receives the death benefit, which would ordinarily be fully excluded under IRC § 101(a)(1). However, since the policy was transferred for valuable consideration, the benefits are taxable to T, the purchaser. T can

exclude only the amounts of consideration paid upon the initial transfer plus any premiums subsequently.

v.   Interest payments on insurance benefits: IRC § 101(c)

IRC § 101(c) held after the death of the insured are included in Beneficiary's GI.

vi.   Proceeds Payable after Death: IRC § 101(d)

IRC § 101(d) provides that where proceeds are payable after the death of the insured, only a portion of each payment must be excluded. In effect, this provision permits the recipient beneficiary to construct an exclusion ratio to be applied against payments received after the death of the insured. The amount excludable represents the death benefit of the insurance policy. The amount excluded represents interest on such payments.

The difference between IRC § 101(c) and IRC § 101(d) applies where the amount of principle is kept relatively intact while the interest paid is a separate and distinguishable sum. In IRC § 101(d), in contrast, each payment consists of a mixture of principle and interest payments.

Example 1:
A dies. The death benefit on the policy of insurance on his life is $100,000. B (beneficiary), asks that the company hold the policy for a period of 10 years and collects interest during that period. The insurance proceeds are fully excludable under IRC § 101(a), while the interest is clearly taxable under IRC § 101(c).

Example 2:
If, on the facts of the previous example, B and the insurer agree that the insurer would pay to B $200,000 over a period of 10 years, each payment would consist of 50% principle and 50% interest.

h.   Property transferred in connection with performance of services: IRC § 83

When property is transferred to a person who has provided services, the recipient must include the Fair Market Value (FMV) (determined without regard to any restriction other than a restriction which by its terms will never lapse), the recognition of income occurs "at the first time the rights of the person having the beneficial interest in such property are:

i.   transferable;
ii.   not subject to a substantial risk of forfeiture, whichever first occurs. Any amount paid by the service provider reduced the amount includible:

Example: Tom, a real estate salesman, is responsible for putting together a large (and profitable) transaction. To reward his efforts, his employer, a real estate broker, waives its commission on a parcel of property worth $100,000 which Tom wants to purchase for his personal use. The amount of the commission waived is $6,000. Tom has $6,000 of compensation income under IRC §§61(a)(1) and §83(a). the $6,000 amount is included in Tom's income in the year in which the purchase occurs, since the property is fully transferable by Tom and there is no risk of forfeiture encumbering the acquisition of the property. If Tom sold soap instead of real estate, and his employer rewarded his efforts with stock options worth $6,000, the result would be the same as in the previous example, unless the employer conditioned the option so that if Tom no longer was employed by the manufacturer of soap at the end of a three year period, stock purchased with the options would have to be returns to the manufacturer. The value of the option would not be included in tom's gross income, until the condition had either been satisfied or expired, since the possibility of having to return the stock constituted a substantial risk of forfeiture.

i.   Transferability of property.

IRC § 83(c)(2): Transferability of property: rights of a person in property are transferable only if rights are not subject to substantial risk of forfeiture. Denial of ability to sell or transfer.

ii.   Substantial risk of forfeiture.

IRC § 83(c)(1) Substantial risk of forfeiture: If person's right to full enjoyment of property is conditioned on the future performance of substantial services by any individual.

Does inclusion under IRC § 83 always result in ordinary income? The answer is "no." IRC §83(b) provides a (sometimes) useful alternative: to make an election to include the value of the option in gross income *currently*, notwithstanding the substantial risk of forfeiture. This election requires the service provider to include the fair market value of the option as ordinary income in the year in which the option is received and the election made. However, no further income is realized when the option vests. Furthermore, when the service provider eventually sells the stock obtained with the option, he will realize *long-term capital gain,* rather than ordinary income.

Caution: If the §83(b) election is so good, why doesn't everybody use it? There are two principal reasons: (1) the election is irrevocable, except upon the consent of the commissioner, who grants such consent only where the transferee is under a mistake of fact as to the ongoing transaction and the revocation must be requested within 60 days of the date on which the mistake of fact first becomes known (Reg. §1.83-2(f)); and (2) if the property obtained with the exercise of the option is subsequently forfeited, no deduction is allowed. IRC §83(b)(1).

Armantrout v. Comm'r, 67 T.C. 996 (1977), aff'd., 570 F.2d 210 (7th Cir. 1978).
Employer made payments to an educational benefit trust. The funds from the trust were only available for college expenses of employee's children.
Held: These payments were simply substitutes for salary and were taxable to the employee at the time the payments were made to the employee's child. Thus, the money was included in the employee's GI even though it was the child, not the father who benefited.

However, the issue to be decided is still fact-sensitive. The employer who wishes to benefit its employees has two clear options: (1) create an educational assistance plan (EAP), which can provide up to $5,250 of educational assistance to employees their spouses and dependents on a non-discriminatory basis, regardless of the fact that the employer was motivated principally by selfish motives in establishing and maintaining the Plan; and (2) if properly motivated, i.e., if proceeding with a "detached and disinterested generosity, a generous employer can establish, *in addition to or in place of the somewhat limited benefits available through an EAP*, a "pure," "no strings attached" scholarship under IRC §117.

The recipient of the services performed must include the full fair market value (FMV) of the property in his income in the year he received the services (child's education), unless the property is either not transferable or is subject to substantial risk of forfeiture. *See Old Colony Trust supra,* for principle that taxable benefit can be realized, even though not physically received.

Example:

A portion of an employees compensation package includes right to buy stock, but only after a one year period, at $100,000 with a FMV (Fair Market Value) of $120,000.

Analysis:

* The $20,000 discount is not currently included in GI.
* Employee must claim as income after restrictions have been lifted, at the FMV at time restriction if lifted less the amount paid for the stock (defers taxation)

Note:

* IRC §83 general rule is that property is still considered property of the transferor until restrictions are lifted. The rationale is that it is not fair to tax an employee until the stock is held free and clear.
* In an IRC §83 environment, the employer's deduction for compensation paid depends on what the employee does, i.e., the employer's deduction is matched to the employer's taxable year in which or with which the employee includes the value of the property transferred in return for services. IRC §83(h).

Teschner v. Comm'r., 38 T.C. 1003 (1962),

A child won a prize and the father, not the child, was taxed.

Held: A prize is a one-time event and is not a substitute for a salary. Additionally, since it was not a salary situation, there was no chance to bargain out the terms.

B. Loans

1. Loans Defined

* A loan may be thought of as a sum which the borrower expects to repay either at a date specified in the future (a term loan) or upon the demand of the lender, (a demand loan) which is evidenced by a promissory note or other acknowledgment of the borrower's obligation to repay. Some loans are secured by assets of the borrower while others are unsecured.

2. Loans explained

* Amounts borrowed from a lender are not included in the borrower's gross income. This is due to the fact that, apart from the opportunities made available by a secure funding source, a *true* borrower is not considered to have realized the proceeds of the loan. A borrower in a *true loan situation* does not derive the appropriate economic benefit from the proceeds for a real loan because he is genuinely obligated to repay the amount of the loan when due. Moreover, "real loans" ordinarily accrue "adequate" interest on a daily basis.

* Interest paid to the lender is income to the lender.

* Interest paid by a borrower may or may not be deductible by the borrower. IRC §§163(h)(1). In the case of a taxpayer other than a corporation, "personal interest" paid or accrued during the taxable year is not deductible. "Personal interest" includes such items as interest payable on a car loan, credit card debt, clothing, food, etc. It is in contrast to commercial debt, which is paid or accrued in a profit making activity (IRC §212) or in a trade or business of the taxpayer. IRC §162. A major exception to the foregoing limitation on personal interest is "qualified residence interest" within IRC §163(h).

At times, it may be unclear whether the taxpayer who ends up with the cash is actually a borrower or a thief. This invariably involves a question of fact, viz., whether the "borrower" was actually that or, instead was a thief.

Gilbert v. Commissioner, 552 F.2d 478 (2d. Cir. 1977).
The president of a company took money for personal purposes, apparently intending to pay it back.

Held: Even though this was an unratified transaction (without board approval), it was more like a loan and less like a "simple taking." In the former case, the amount received by the taxpayer was not income. Whereas in the latter case, it is.

Comm'r. v. Indianapolis Power and Light, 88 T.C. 964 (1987).
Deposits required from high risk customers to ensure future payment were considered security deposits and not gross income because the customer maintained control over the funds characterized as security deposits.

C. Welfare, social security and unemployment compensation Benefits

In general, all payments received by an employee in an employment context are presumed to be taxable, unless "otherwise provided." Special rules do exist for social security and unemployment benefit compensation benefits.

1. Welfare payments received:
* are not included as GI
* are not considered in the IRC under Section 61

2. Social security: **IRC § 86**.

Partially taxable:
* "Social security benefits" are only partially taxed. IRC §86(a). An amount equal to 50% of social security benefits received is taxable if the taxpayer's modified Adjusted Gross Income (AGI) (i.e. any amount received by a taxpayer) has a monthly benefit under Title II of the social security code or a "tier 1," when retirement benefit exceeds the base amount (i.e. $32,000 on a joint return, $25,000 for an individual). IRC § 86(a)(1); IRC § 86(b)(1) and (b)(2).

* An amount equal to 85% of social security benefits received is taxable if the taxpayers AGI exceeds the adjusted base amount of $44,000 on a joint return or $34,000 for an individual. IRC § 86(a)(2); § 86(c)

3. Unemployment compensation: **IRC § 85**

IRC § 85(a) provides that "unemployment compensation" is taxable. For this purpose "unemployment compensation" is any amount received under a federal or state law which is "in the nature of unemployment compensation."

Comment: This rule makes sense. Unemployment compensation is really wage replacement. It is a substitute for income and therefore should be taxed like that for which it substitutes.

D. IMPUTED INCOME.

1. Imputed Income Defintion: **IRC § 61**.
"Imputed income" is a phrase developed by economists to describe the economic benefit as income derived from the value of a skill for the ownership of property. In a nutshell, if one own his own house, he does not have to pay rent. If one has a legal skill, he does not have to hire a lawyer to represent him. In each case, the economic benefit is derived from the relief of an obligation of the taxpayer.

In the U.S. tax system imputed income is not taxed. However, one must distinguish between imputed income, which is not taxable, and direct income which is taxed.

2. Imputed Income Illustration.

Example 1:
If an employer and employee enter into an employment contract. The employer undertakes to pay a salary and to also pay the employee's federal tax obligations or medical bills.
Both the salary and the amount of taxes or bills paid constitute income to the employee under Old Colony Trust v. Comm'r., discussed *supra*. where the employer paid the employee's tax obligation pursuant to an employment contract. The amounts were found to be compensatory and thus, taxable to the employee even though paid to a third party.

Example 2:
Wiring one's own house instead of working overtime to pay someone to wire one's house is not a taxable benefit to the homeowner. It is her house and her skill, rather than that of a third party such as the homeowner's employer, who brings about the benefit.

Contra: A real estate broker, who is able to buy property at a discount because he doesn't have to pay a real estate commission, is being compensated for his services. The taxable benefit is measured by the value of what he doesn't have to pay, namely the commission.

The proper way to view this is to treat each taxpayer as though he received payment for his services in the form of cash. This should then be used to procure the benefit provided by the other taxpayer. Rev. Rul. 79-24, 1979-1 C.B. 60 Thus reconstructed, the taxable benefit is clear.

E.   BARTER

Revenue Ruling 79-24, 1979-1 C.B.60 reaffirms the rule that imputed income is not taxable. However, it also affirms the rule that taxable income can result from a non-cash benefit provided by a third party.

Example:
A landlord receives a work of art from a professional artist in return for allowing the artist to use an apartment for six months rent-free. Any economic benefits derived by either taxpayer prior to the agreement regarding the apartment would be classified as imputed income and not subject to tax under the present U.S. system. However, when the parties exchanged the use of property for a work of art, each has a taxable exchange. Such transactions are called "barter" transactions and are taxable if commercial goods or services are involved.

F .   GIFTS, PRIZES AND AWARDS

1. Gifts and inheritances: IRC § 102

IRC § 102(a) GI does not include the value of any property, whether cash or non-cash, acquired through gift, bequest, devise or inheritance.
* It is the motive of the Donor that determines whether a transaction is a gift.
* Transfer must be made out of *detached and disinterested generosity* or out of affection, respect, admiration, charity or like impulses.

IRC § 102(b) Exclusion is specifically limited. It does not apply to income derived from gifted property or to gifts of the income itself from property. Such gifts are taxable.

IRC §§ 102(c), 102(a)   Exclusion in IRC §102(a) does apply to gifts from employers to employees (in their capacity as employees). *See* Prop. Reg. § 1.102-1(f).

Commissioner v. Duberstein, 363 U.S. 278 (1960),
This case involved two unrelated taxpayers, Duberstein and Berman. Duberstein made frequent business referrals to Berman. Berman, in gratitude and in all probability to keep the flow of referrals coming, acquired a Cadillac for Duberstein, even though there was no contract between them and Duberstein did not expect to be paid.
Held: Duberstein had to include the fair market value of the Cadillac in his gross income in the year in which he received it. Berman did not *give* the Cadillac to Duberstein within the meaning of IRC§102(a). The transfer of the Cadillac was not prompted by detached and *disinterested generosity*. Instead it was intended by Berman either as compensation for past services rendered (the referrals) and anticipation of future services (future referrals).

The question of whether a transfer is motivated by detached and disinterested "generosity" within the meaning of IRC § 102(a) is a question of fact. The key factor is the primary motive that prompted the transferor to make the gift. Factors considered important include: i. the relationship of the parties; ii. the existence of a business relationship; iii. whether there is any moral or legal obligation for the transfer.

2.   Prizes and awards: **IRC § 74.**
Except as provided in IRC § 117 [scholarships] GI includes amounts received as prizes and awards. *See Rogallo v. U.S.*, 475 F. 2d 1 (4th Cir. 1973).

Two exceptions:

IRC § 74(b). GI does not include amounts received in recognition of: Religious, charitable, scientific, artistic, literary or civic achievement if:
  i.   Selected without any action on his own to control, and There are no requirements for substantial future services as a condition of receipt, or
  ii. Recipient gives the prize or award away to a government or organization. IRC § 170(c).

IRC § 74(c). GI does not include employee achievement awards if the cost to the employer does not exceed the amount allowable as a deduction to the employer under IRC § 274(j).
*   If the amount does exceed the deduction, GI includes the greater of the excess in cost to the employer over the deduction or the excess in value of the award over the deduction.

3.   Rental value of parsonage: IRC § 107.
In the case of a "minister of the gospel," the rental value of a home furnished to the minister as part of compensation or rental allowance paid as compensation may be excluded from the minister's gross income.

G. CAPITAL APPRECIATION, BASIS RECOVERY and REALIZATION

1.   Computation of Basis, Gain or Loss

a.   Gains from Dealings in Property. **IRC § 61(a)(3).**
Include in GI gains derived from dealings in property.
The word "dealings" is sufficiently broad that it encompasses all the ways in which a taxpayer can "close out" an investment in a particular property, including sales, exchanges and "other" dispositions. See IRC § 1001.

b.   Determination of Amount of Gain or Loss Realize and/or Recognized: **IRC § 1001**

"Amount Realized" is the total value of money and other property "received" by the taxpayer in the transaction.

Note: The "amount realized" includes indirect benefits, such as assumptions of taxpayers indebtedness. *See Crane v. Comm'r.*, 331 U.S. 1 (1947).

Gain or loss is the amount realized (sale price) less adjusted basis (cost). Any gain or loss realized is generally recognized (i.e., any realized gain or loss must be reported in the taxable year in which the event giving rise to the realization occurs).

Example:
A purchases building for $200 with a promissory note, secured by a mortgage on the building.
Basis = $200. Building appreciates in value to $300 and A sells.

Analysis:
Buyer pays $100 in cash and assumes the $200 liability. Under IRC § 1001, gain is excess of amount realized over basis. Amount Realized = $300, which includes the amount of liability assumed by the buyer (*Crane v. Comm'r.*, 331 U.S. 1 (1947)). In general, *basis* represents the taxpayer's net costs for obtaining the property, (i.e., the sum of cash, the fair market value of property other than cash and any "acquisition debt," paid for the property less depreciation plus any capital improvements made after acquisition).

"Realization" - Before any increase in net worth becomes taxable a realization must occur, *Cottage Savings v. Comm'r.*, 499 U.S. 554 (1991).

    i.   Conversion of Property into Cash.

Reg. § 1.001-1 Conversion of property into cash is realization, and the exchange of property for property materially different in kind or extent is realization as well.

    A) Realization on property: gain /loss occurs only on the sale or other disposition of the property:
    * "Borrowing Out" or Securing Debt with a mortgage is not realization. *Woodsam Associates Inc. v. Comm'r.*, 198 F.2d 357 (2d Cir. 1952).
    * Offer is not realization
    * Exchange is realization if the property received " differs materially either in kind or in extent from property given up" Reg. § 1.1001-1(a), *Cottage Savings v. Comm'r.*, 499 U.S. 1 (1991).

    B) Amount Realized: Sum of money plus FMV of any other property received by the taxpayer on the transaction
    * Mortgaged Property: TP's amount realized is money plus the amount of any debt secured by the property for which TP is no longer liable.

1) (*Crane* Rule) : Seller realizes full amount of liability, even though not personally liable.

2) Where property is worth less than the outstanding balance on the loan (mortgage), TP nonetheless realizes the full amount of non-recourse loan then outstanding. *Comm'r. v. Tufts* 461 U.S. 300 (1983).

3) Non-recourse liability (NRL) v. Recourse liability:

   a) **Non-Recourse Liability**: TP realizes full amount of debt when she disposes of property, where the debt is: (i) paid off; or (ii) liability is assumed by purchaser; or (iii) property is acquired "Subject To" debt. Liability is treated as part of sales price. Thus any gain which results will be treated as capital gain, subject to the rules regarding depreciation recapture, if the property disposed of was a capital asset.

   b) **Recourse liability**: Where debtor is personally liable for recourse debt, his personal assets may be seized to fully satisfy debt after collateral is taken. The amount taken by creditors is treated as ordinary income, not capital because it does not result from a sale or exchange.

ii. Conversion of Property into Cash.

Reg. § 1.1001-2: Where the amount of the indebtedness exceeds the FMV of the property which secures it, and the property is surrendered in cancellation of the debt, the "Amount Realized" by the debtor is limited to the FMV of the property. The portion of the debt in excess of the value of the property is considered to be a discharge of indebtedness income IRC § 61(a)(12). Thus, only the position of the debt which has been "sold or exchanged" can qualify as capital gain.

Example:
Owner (T) of property with Basis of $4,000. It has a $9,000 debt secured by a mortgage and FMV of $8,100. T transfers property to Purchaser (P).

A) If NRL: T has capital gain of $5,000 because he is treated as having realized the full ($9,000) amount of the debt.

B) If RL: T has a capital gain of $4,100, which is attributable to the excess of the FMV of the property, $8,100, *less* T's basis in the property, $4,000. The additional $9,000 of debt is viewed as having been "forgiven" by P, the purchaser, but is not attributable to a "sale or exchange". Consequently this amount is ordinary income, regardless of the nature of the property. T could exclude ordinary income if he were insolvent (*Comm'r. v. Tufts*, 461 U.S. 300 (1983).

2. Basis of property-cost: **IRC § 1012**

*   Provides that the basis of purchased property is cost unless otherwise provided (see IRC § 1016 for post-acquisition adjustments).

*   Where property is received in exchange for services, the Basis in the property acquired is the FMV of the property received. Reg. § 1.61-2(d)(2)(i).

*   Cost includes "Acquisition Debt" (i.e. the indebtedness to acquire or substantially improve the property). IRC § 163(h)(3)(B).

*   The cost basis does not include contingent liability that might never be paid. *Estate of Franklin v. Comm'r.*, 544 F.2d 1045 (9th Cir. 1976).

*   Limited obligation depends on facts and circumstances.

*   Purchase Expense: Brokers and Attorney's fees are added to Basis.

*   Option Cost is added to basis in property acquired upon exercise of the option.

Comm'r. v. Tufts, 461 U.S. 300 (1983)
The cost basis of the property under IRC § 1012 is the full cost of the property, including any part of that cost paid for with borrowed funds. That is, when property is acquired subject to debt, the buyer is treated as though he had received cash equal to the amount of the debt and had used that cash to buy the property.

However, where the purchase price is not approximately equivalent to the fair market value of the property, payments on the "debt" will not yield equity to the purchaser or where the debt is otherwise speculative or contingent, the debt may be disregarded in calculating the taxpayer's basis in the property. *See Estate of Franklin v. Comm'r.*, 863 F.2d 263 (3d Cir. 1988).

Under *Crane*, a taxpayer's basis in property consists of the amount of cash, the fair market value of any property contributed in as taxable exchange and the amount of "acquisition debt" assumed or otherwise incurred as part of the acquisition of the property. *Crane v. Comm'r., 331 U.S. 1 (1947)*.

* *Crane* treats recourse and non-recourse liabilities the same.

* However, both *Franklin* and *Pleasant Summit* limit the purchaser's basis "when it appears that the debt has economic significance only if the property substantially appreciates in value prior to the date at which a very large portion of the purchase price is to be discharged. Under these circumstances the purchaser has not secured "the use or forbearance of money" (Estate of Franklin).

* In *Pleasant Summit*, Tax Court Judge Cohen followed *Odand'hal v. Comm'r.*, 748F.2d 908, 912-14 (4th Cir. 1984) *cert. den'd., 471 U.S. 1143 (1985)*. Odand'hal and its progeny stand for the preposition that non-recourse debt in excess of fair market value is not to be included in the cost of property for purposes of calculating the deduction. Ultimately, Judge Cohen limited the taxpayer's basis in the property which was acquired at an inflated price to the fair market value of the property plus the amount of cash paid.

3. Adjustments to Basis: **IRC § 1016.**
The taxpayer's adjusted basis includes his/her initial basis *plus* the cost of the post-acquisition improvements (capital expenditures) *less* any basis "recovered" by way of depreciation amortization or depletion. IRC § 1016.

The taxpayer's initial basis depends on how the property was acquired. If the property was purchased, the basis is cost (IRC § 101(2)). If the property was given (gifted) to the taxpayer, her basis will be a "carry-over" of the donor's basis (IRC § 101(2)). In contrast, if the property was inherited, the initial basis should be the fair market value (FMV) for estate tax purposes. (IRC § 101(4)).
* Calculation of Basis.
* *Crane* treats recourse and non-recourse alike (*Crane v. Comm'r.*, 331 U.S. 1 (1947)).

*   *Franklin* says that if non-recourse liability exceeds the fair market value (FMV) at acquisition, take the FMV as basis (Estate of Franklin v. Comm'r., 544 F.2d 1045 (9th Cir. 1976).

*   *Pleasant Summit* holds that non-recourse liability is limited to FMV plus cash paid (Pleasant Summit Land Corp. v. Comm'r., 863 F.2d 263 (3d Cir. 1988)).

Example 1:
FMV = $1,500
Cash paid $1,000 and $1,000 *recourse* loan
(Equity = $500) Basis = $2,000 (taxpayer has incentive not to walk away, but to stay and pay loan because if TP stays and pays the loan, loss = $500 but if TP walks away loss = $1,000).

(Unless limited, a taxpayer has incentive to inflate purchase price and thereby inflate depreciable basis without increasing personal liability, since debt is on a nonrecourse basis. Under *Estate of Franklin* and *Pleasant Summit Land Corp.*, a taxpayer's basis in property is limited to fair market value plus, under *Pleasant Summit* analysis, the amount of cash actually paid by the taxpayer).

Example 2:
FMV = $1,500
Cash paid $1,000 and $1,000 *nonrecourse* loan
(Equity = $500) Incentive to stay and pay loan exists because same result as in example (1)
Basis = $1,500
Under *Pleasant*, basis = $2,500 FMV plus cash paid

Woodsam Associates, Inc. v. Comm'r., 198 F. 2d 357 (2d Cir. 1952).
Issue: Is borrowing against land a realization event?
A principle that is especially important to owners of real estate is that the "mortgaging out" of property (i.e., borrowing against the owner's equity in the real estate, is not a taxable event). Consequently no gain or loss is realized and none therefore can be recognized. This is a corollary to the Crain rule that acquisition debt is added to the taxpayer's basis in property. Since the obligation to repay the loan is genuine, the taxpayer is not taxable on the receipt of the loan proceeds, even though they may exceed the taxpayer's basis in the property.

4. Basis in property acquired from a decedent ("Step-Up" or "Step-Down"): **IRC § 1014.**

Basis of property "acquired from a decedent" is the FMV of the property for estate tax purposes. Thus, fair market value is measured either at the time of the decedent's death or, if the alternate valuation date is elected, six months after the date of death.

* Due to the fact that the beneficiary's basis is adjusted to fair market value, the amount of capital gain (or *loss*) is erased.

Note: The FMV Basis Rule does not apply where property was acquired by decedent within 1 year of death and then reacquired by the person from whom the decedent acquired it, or his/her spouse IRC § 1014(e).

Example:
T's aunt dies on July 1, year 1 at the age of 100. Six months earlier, her granddaughter G.D. had given her a "Vienna regulator," an antique clock which was worth several thousand dollars more that she had paid for it some years before. D had admired the clock from the moment that G.D. brought it home. G.D., sensing that her grandmother's life was drawing to a close, gave it to her as a gesture that she felt would make her grandmother comfortable in her last days.
If D leaves the clock to G.D. in her will, the ordinary rule of IRC § 1014(a) will not operate. Instead, G.D.'s basis will be determined by reference to D's basis, which of course is determined by reference to D's cost of the "Vienna regulator".

Note: The result in the forgoing example would be the same if G.D. were motivated entirely by a desire to minimize capital gain on her subsequent reacquisition of the property. Of course, the converse is true as well. If D survives more than one year from the time she acquires the property from G.D., IRC § 1014(e) cannot, by its own terms, apply. Thus, whether G.D. is motivated by a desire to help her grandmother or, instead, a desire to lower her capital gains tax liability, IRC § 1014(e) affords the advantages of a "bright-line" rule, which dispenses with the need to establish the motives of the initial transfer.

5. In a community property state BOTH shares are "Stepped-Up:" **IRC § 1014(b)(9).**

Note:
* Unrealized appreciation is not subject to income tax, simply because the owner of the property has died.

* Heirs are not subject to the increase in value, from the donor's original basis.
* If spouses own property jointly, only the deceased spouse's share of the property gets Stepped-Up. The surviving Spouse's share gets no adjustment. It was not "acquired from a decedent." The stepped up basis is, 1/2 of the original basis plus the current FMV of the property (IRC § 1014(a)(9).

6. Basis of property acquired by gifts and transfers in trust:
   IRC § 1015.

Where property is acquired by gift there is a transfer during the life of the transferor rather then inherited. Thus, the Step-Up/Step-Down (IRC § 1014) rule does not apply. Instead, the donee "carries over" the donor's historic basis rather than the fair market value of the property at the time of the gift. This is consistent with the concept that a gift of property is not an income taxable event to the donor. Thus, after the gift, the potential tax consequences of the property also *carry-over to the donee.*

Example:
Donor buys property for $100. Donor holds until it is worth $1,000, at which point she gives it to her niece. Gift to donee (niece) is not treated as a "sale or other disposition" of the gifted property and the donor does not realize the $900 gain on the gifted property. However, the gain is not eliminated, rather it is deferred and carried over with the gifted property to the donee who now holds the property having a FMV of $1000, with an adjusted basis of $100.

Taft v. Bowers, 278 U.S. 470 (1929)
Facts: Father purchased $1,000 in the shares of stock of a particular company. He gave the stock to his daughter when its fair market value equaled $2,000. Daughter later sells the stock for $5,000 and pays tax on the gain in value which occurred after she took possession.
Held: The daughter's basis is $1,000, which is determined by reference to the father's basis.

7. Loss Limitation Rule.

IRC § 1015(a) provides that where the value of gifted property has declined while held by the donor, the amount of "built-in-loss" is not transferable to the donee where the donee subsequently sells at a loss.

Example 1:
Assume the same facts as in the preceding example above except that the donor paid $1000, and the property is only worth $100 now. If the donee (Niece) sells the property for $80 the deductible loss is $20 *not* $920.

Example 2:
Same facts, the donee (niece) holds the property long enough for the market to turn around. She sells for $1,100. The rule of carry-over basis says the donee's basis would now would be $1000. (The Loss Limitation Rule limits the loss, it is not gain enhancing).

IRC § 1015(d)(6) Donor's basis to be adjusted UPWARD to reflect that portion of any gift tax paid which is proportionate to the net appreciation of the value of the property.

Example 3:
Using the facts of the gift to donee (niece) described above and assuming the gift tax paid was $150, the donee's basis would be $1,135, which is determined by adding $1,000 and $135. [$900/$1000 (9/10) X $150 = $135].

H. ANNUITIES

* Annuity is a contract in which taxpayer invests a fixed sum, whether paid in a lump sum or in installments, which is later paid back with interest at regular intervals for a predetermined period or for life of the annuitant.
* An annuity is a pool to which one contributes money and from which, after a specified time, one can withdraw money. The winners are the people who live the longest.
* Insurance company extracts a fee and ensures that the money remains as long as the contributors live.
* Typical deal is for the company to agree to provide benefits either for a fixed term of years or a period determined by 1 or more lives such as the annuitant and her spouse.
* Statute provides method of allocating what should be tax free: "the taxpayer's own capital" and that which is not tax free is the amount received in excess of the annuitant's investment.
* The part of each payment that represents the taxpayer's investment in the contract is exempt as a return of capital.

*   The balance is treated as taxable interest which represents ordinary income to the taxpayer.

1.   Annuities; certain proceeds of endowments and life insurance contracts: **IRC § 72**

   a.   Scope of Annuity Included in GI: **IRC § 72(a)**
   GI includes any amount received as an annuity payment under an annuity, life insurance contract or endowment.

   b.   Exclusion Ratio: **IRC § 72(b)**
   Annuity payments are only partially taxed notwithstanding.
   *   The exclusion ratio represents the amount of each payment that is considered a partial recovery of the initial investment.
   *   This amount is tax free.
   *   The balance is taxable.

   The Exclusion Ratio is simply the amount of the annuitant's investment divided by the expected return . The product of this calculation is a percentage or ratio which is applied to each payment received as nontaxable recovery of capital, and the balance received is treated as ordinary income.

   Example:
   A, age 45, pays $150,000 in a lump sum to a company that specializes in annuity policies. The company agrees to pay $30,000 per year for A's life, commencing when he reaches age 55. If A has a 15 year life expectancy at age 55, he will exclude $10,000, (1/3) of each payment from his income. However, the balance $20,000, (2/3) will represent ordinary income.

   $$\text{Exclusion Ratio} = \frac{\text{Investment in Contract (150,000)}}{\text{Expected Return (450,000)}} = \frac{1}{3}$$
   (15 years X $30,000 per year)

   The portion received which is excluded is limited to the amount of money paid into the plan.

   If the annuitant dies before the investment in the contract is fully recovered, A deduction is allowed for the shortfall IRC §72(b)(3)(A). This deduction is treated as a net operating loss IRC §72(b)(3)(C). *See* Net Operating Losses, Claims of Right, Tax Benefit Rule,*infra*.

If the contract provides for payments to be made to another person, that person can take the deduction for the taxable year in which such payments are received. IRC § 72(b)(3)(B).

The deduction is treated as if it were attributable to the trade or business of the taxpayer. IRC § 72(c)(3)(C).

c.   Adjustment in Investment **IRC § 72(c).**

     i.   Investment in the contract is the aggregate amount of premiums or other consideration paid for the contract minus the aggregate amount previously received under the contract to the extent that the amount was excluded from GI.

     ii.   Adjustment in Investment where there is a refund feature if the expected return depends on the life expectancy of one or more individuals and the contract provides for payments to be made to one or more beneficiaries after the death of the annuitant and such payments are in the nature of a refund of the consideration paid, then the value of the refund feature must be subtracted from the amount of investment in the contract, determined in paragraph one.

     iii.   Annuity Starting date is the first day of the first period for which an amount was received as an annuity unless it was before Jan 1, 1954, in which case that is the starting date.

I.   DISCHARGE OF INDEBTEDNESS

1.   Income from Discharge of Indebtedness

IRC § 61(a)(12) GI includes a taxpayer's Gross Income and any increases in the TP's wealth due to a discharge of the TP's indebtedness.

IRC § 108 Income from discharge of indebtedness
Provides a number of important exceptions to the general rule established by IRC § 61(a)(12).

Note:
Where discharge of taxpayer's debt is accomplished with a "detached and disinterested generosity," the resulting increase in TP's wealth is *NOT* part of TP's Gross Income, because it is a gift under IRC § 102, 108 (a).

Note Also: Employer paying employee's income tax is income to the employee taxpayer whose debt is forgiven.

Donor must pay gift tax. If donee agrees to pay gift tax, then Donor has a discharge of his obligation to pay the gift tax which is treated as an amount realized on a partial sale of the property. Under this analysis a portion of the property is considered to have been gifted.

IRC §108(a)(1) GI does not include any amount *which would otherwise be included in GI* due to discharge of taxpayer's indebtedness if
a) The discharge is in a bankruptcy case (Title 11 IRC § 108(a)(1)(A)); *or*
b) The discharge occurred while the taxpayer was insolvent (Liability is greater than the FMV of taxpayer's assets)(IRC §§ 108(a)(1)(B) and (d)(3))
    Note: Exclusion is limited to the extent of insolvency (IRC § 108(a)(3)); *or*
c) The indebtedness is a qualified farm indebtedness (IRC §§ 108(a)(1)(C), 108(g))
    Note: To qualify:
    *   the debt must have been incurred directly in the operation of the taxpayer's trade or business of farming;
    *   for the three prior taxable years, at least 50% of the aggregate gross revenues must be derived from farming (IRC § 108 (g)); *or*
d) The indebtedness discharged is "Qualified Real Property Business Indebtedness" (IRC § 108(c)(3)) and the taxpayer is a qualified "pass-through entity (i.e. Sub. S Corporation, Partnership, or LLC/LLP).

IRC §108(b) If discharge is excluded from GI under subparagraph (a), "tax attributes" of taxpayer must be reduced. "Attributes" include, net operating loss, capital loss and general business credit carry-overs, the minimum tax credit available under IRC § 53 will be in general business credit carry-overs, the minimum tax credit or the taxpayer's basis in depreciable property (IRC § 108 (b)) and IRC § 1017). *See* IRC §§ 172, 121, carry-overs.

IRC §108(d)(1) Indebtedness exists either when the taxpayer is liable or when TP holds property subject to an indebtedness.

Note:
*   Discharge of Indebtedness is income because the taxpayer's net worth is increased. *See Kirby Lumber v. U.S.*, 284 U.S. 1 (1931).

* If debt is discharged by a gift of the creditor, then it is a gift, not income.
* Loans where there is a genuine obligation to repay, are not considered income due to the repayment
* If employer gives an employee money to pay back a loan, then discharge is most likely included in employee's revenue in form of indirect compensation. (See Old Colony Trust Co. v Comm'r., 279 U.S. 716 (1929).

Kirby Lumber v. U.S., 284 U.S.1 (1931)
Kirby issued bonds for $12,000,000, later that year it bought back bonds rated at $1 million for approximately $862,000.
Held: Corporation had income from a discharge of indebtedness. this resulted in accession to wealth, therefore Kirby should be taxed.
The excess of issuing price over repurchase price is gain and is included in GI.

Zarin v. Comm'r., 916 F.2d 110 (3d Cir. 1990)
Taxpayer had a $3.4 million gambling debt. Casino violated State (NJ) gambling statute by increasing TP's credit line after told to stop. As a result, debt was unenforceable. TP settled with the resort for a sum substantially less than actually owed. Commissioner argued that TP had a Kirby-like "accession" measured by the difference in the amount paid between the debt and the settlement.
Held: The debt was the amount ($500,000) on which the parties agreed (product of the arm's-length negotiation). The "debt" alleged by IRS, was unenforceable due to violation of state law by the casino. This was not "property" held by taxpayer. IRC § 108(d)(1)(a),(b).

2. Part Sale/Part Gift Transactions
Code makes no direct provision for part sales/part gifts, but, Reg. § 1.101-1(e) and Reg. § 1.1015-4 set out the basic rules. As the "donor" has a taxable gain to the extent of the amount realized (the amount of gift tax paid by the donee that exceeds the adjusted basis in the property). The donee, on the other hand, has a basis equal to the greater of what he pays in taxes or the carry-over basis of the donor.

Donor gain = gift tax - adjusted basis

Diedrich v. Comm'r., 457 U.S. 191 (1982)
Donor of property whose gift tax liability is paid by the donee realizes taxable income to the extent that the gift tax paid exceeds the donor's adjusted basis.
Held: Treat as if the property was sold for the amount of the gift tax.

In contrast, if parent pays child's income tax liability, it is likely to be a gift.

IRC § 2502(d) imposes the obligation of paying gift tax on the donor. Nevertheless, donee may be compelled to pay tax as a transferee. See IRC § 6324.

At times, a donor will require the donee to agree to pay the gift tax as a condition of the gift. This technique has come to be known as the "net gift" and the donee's promise is treated as consideration furnished for the transfer.

Since 1982, when the supreme court decided *Diedrich v. Comm'r.,* 457 US 191 (1982), a gift involves both income and gift tax consequences. Under Reg. § 1.1001-1(e), the donor has a taxable gain to the extent that the gift tax obligation undertaken by the donee exceeds the donors adjusted basis in the gifted property. Conversely, the donee has a basis in the gifted property equal to *the greater of:* (i) the amount the donee paid for the property; i.e., the amount of gift tax paid; or (ii) a carry-over of the donor's basis in the property.

3. IRC § 165(d) Wagering losses

Wagering losses shall be allowed only to the extent of the gains from such transactions. See "Personal Losses" IRC § 165 and § 469.

J. ILLEGAL INCOME

* Since 1969, with the exception of specific statutory provisions, such as IRC §§ 162(c), (f) and (g), there is no "public policy" obstacle to deducting the expenses of an illicit trade or business. In fact, IRC § 162 does not distinguish between legal or non-legal businesses
* Expenses for illegal activities that are not in themselves inherently illegal are deductible. Comm'r. v. Sullivan, 356 U.S. 27 (1958). *But see* IRC § 280E, discussed, *infra.*

Stephens v. Comm'r., 93 TC 108 (1989); rev'd. and remanded, 905 F.2d 667(2dCir 1990),.
Employee defrauded employer of $1 million. He reported the money on his tax return. When the employee was compelled to return the money by court order, he sought to deduct the amount repaid.
Held: Restitution was neither a fine nor a penalty within IRC § 162(f). Public policy was not offended by allowing a deduction under IRC
If not allowed, there would be a double sting. IRC § 162((f) disallows a deduction for a fine or penalty paid to a government for the violation of any law. Section was inapplicable, because this was not a fine or a penalty.

1. Expenditures in connection with the illegal sale of drugs: IRC § 280E.
Disallows all deductions or credits, otherwise allowable for any amount paid or incurred during the taxable year in carrying on a trade or business the activities of which consist of trafficking in controlled substances within the meaning of Schedule I and II of the Controlled Substance Act, which is prohibited by federal law, or the laws of any state in which such trade or business is conducted.

K. DAMAGES AND INSURANCE PAYMENTS FOR INJURY AND SICKNESS

Example:
A walks down the street holding a valuable vase worth $1000 which he purchased for $100. B, due to his negligence, collides with A and causes him both physical injury and damage to the vase. After a trial, the jury awards A $2,000, allocable $1,000 to the vase and $1,000 to A's physical injury.

Analysis: With regard to the vase, there has been a "sale, exchange, or other disposition," albeit involuntary. The tax consequences of the settlement are that A will have a realized and recognized gain of $900 on the "disposition" of the vase (amount realized = $1,000; basis equals $100); however, due to IRC § 104(a)(2), A will be able to completely exclude the proceeds of the settlement relating to physical injury.

1. Compensation for injuries or sickness: **IRC § 104.**

IRC § 104(a): GI does not include amounts received as compensation for: Workers Compensation (IRC § 104(a)(1)), personal injury or sickness (not only physical)(IRC § 104(a)(2)), accident or health insurance reimbursements (see IRC § 105(b)), except insofar as a deduction for the taxpayer's medical care cost was taken in a prior taxable year (See chapter *infra* Net Operating Losses, Claim of Right, Tax Benefit Rule), pension or annuity resulting from sickness or injury from service in the armed forces or disability income from an approved terrorist attack while engaged in official duties as a U.S. employee outside the U.S.(IRC §§ 104(a)(4) and (5))

* Tax must be paid if punitive damages related to mental suffering or emotional distress of TP
* Damages for personal injuries or sickness are excluded whether paid in a lump sum or in installments (IRC § 104 (a)(2))
* Medical insurance proceeds are included in GI to the extent that the employer paid for the premium which was not included in GI of the employee; *Exception* where proceeds reimburse employee for expense of medical care (IRC § 105(b)); contrast Section 104 of the Code.
* If an individual employee, rather than the employer, pays for the insurance, all benefits from the policy are excluded, unless the tax benefit rule applies. IRC § 104(a)(3). Where the individual is employed and the employer pays the insurance premiums, then the portion of the proceeds attributable to the employer's contribution is

taxable, unless the insurance proceeds reimburse the taxpayer for extensive medical care within IRC § 213. *See* IRC §105(b).

Note:
* Medical expenses recovered, which have not previously been deducted by the taxpayer are non-taxable.
* Punitive damages for non-physical injuries are included in GI § 104(a)(2) (alienation of affection, slander, etc).
* To be excludable, benefits - whether procured by way of tort litigation or by insurance - must compensate for a personal injury and cannot represent a mere wage replacement. IRC § 105(a).
* If a disabled person gets privately compensated or disability insurance in addition to salary replacement, such compensation is not taxable.

Reg § 1.104-1(c) Damages received, whether in a lump sum or as periodic payments and whether by judgment or settlement, on account of personal injury or sickness are excluded. To be excluded the claim must be based on tort like rights.

U.S. v. Burke, 504 U.S. 229 (1992)
Taxpayer was one of several female plaintiffs that were awarded damages attributable to sexual discrimination under Title VII. As it existed at the time of the plaintiffs suit, title vii relief was confined to back pay and an injunction to reinstate the plaintiff in the work force. Taxpayer characterized the award as a non-taxable personal injury under IRC § 104(a)(2), but the Supreme Court disagreed. According to the majority opinion, to be excluded, a personal injury must represent a tort or tort-like recovery. Apparently an essential element of a tort-like recovery is the availability of a broad range of damages, including punitive damages. Although Title VII had been amended by the time of the decision to permit such relief, the Court held, nonetheless, that the plaintiff's recovery was taxable.

Schlier v. Comm'r., 115 S. Ct. 2159 (1995)
Airline pilot sought to exclude damages received on account of age discrimination. Court disagreed finding that the award represented back pay, not a personal injury, and therefore was not excluded. After *Schlier/Burke*, and a small but significant modification of the statute which requires that an injury must be physical to be excludible, the statute also specifies that emotional distress "shall not be treated as a physical injury or physical illness for this purpose the taxpayer must demonstrate a personal physical injury and must have a tort-like claim.

2. Amounts received under accident and health plans:
    IRC § 105.

*   Medical benefits *attributable to employee-provided premiums* which have not previously been deducted (§104(a)(3)), when employer pays premiums, there are no adverse tax consequences on payment of the premiums (IRC §106), but benefits paid by the insurer are taxable, even if not previously deducted by the taxpayer, unless the benefits represent a reimbursement to the taxpayer, his/her spouse or dependents for an expense of "medical care" as that term is broadly construed by IRC §213(d)(1).
*   Employee-paid premiums are not taxable to employee when benefits are received. (IRC § 104(a)(3)).
*   Employer-paid premiums = **not** taxed to employee when paid, but recovery **is** taxed, unless IRC § 105(b) (reimbursement of medical care cost) applies. Tax on recovery after deducting medical expense reimbursement for permanent loss and loss of use.
*   GI does not include compensation for payment for the permanent loss or loss of use of a member or function of a body, or the permanent disfigurement, of the taxpayer, spouse or a dependent, provided the payment is computed without reference to the nature of the injury and without regard to the period the employee is absent from work.
*   GI includes amounts received for loss of compensation due to inability to work.

IRC § 105(a) GI includes amounts received by an employee under accident or health insurance policies to the extent that such amounts were contributed by the employer either directly (self-insurance) or by the payment of premiums to a medical insurance carrier, where the premiums were *not taxed to the employee* when paid (IRC § 106).

IRC § 105(b) GI does not include compensation for medical expenses which are paid directly or indirectly to the taxpayer. This applies to the employee, spouse and dependents and is a very *important exception* to the general rule expressed in IRC § 105(a).

IRC § 105(c) GI does not include amounts that constitute payment for permanent loss or loss of use of a member or function of the body, or the permanent disfigurement of the taxpayer, his spouse or a dependent, if computed with reference to the nature of the injury without regard to the period the employee is absent from work.

IRC § 105(h) provides an important antidiscrimination component for self-insured medical expense reimbursement plans.

In general, employers like to compensate (and motivate) their more highly compensated employees by providing benefits to them which are deductible to the employer and yet not taxable to the employee. IRC § 105(h) limits these opportunities in regard to employer-provided medical plans. If the plan discriminates in favor of the "highly compensated employee," other as to eligibility to participate in the plan or to receive benefits under the plan, the employee in whose favor the discrimination runs will be denied access to IRC § 105(b) with the consequence that when benefits are delivered, they will be taxable.

3. Contributions by employer to accident and health plans:
   IRC § 106.

   * No tax on employer paid premiums.
   * Employer provided health care is excluded from GI but, see IRC §§ 105(a) and (b), which move the time of the realization event from the establishment of the plan or the payment of premiums to the time benefits are provided by the plan to, or on behalf of, an employee, spouse or dependent.

L. TAX EXEMPT INTEREST AND TAX EXPENDITURES

1. Interest on state and local bonds: **IRC § 103.**

State or local Bond = obligation of a state or any political subdivision thereof.
Interest on state or local bonds may be excluded under IRC § 103(a), unless IRC § 103(b) applies.
CAUTION: Taxpayers are not permitted to deduct interest on funds incurred, or combined, to purchase or acquire obligations, the interest of which is wholly exempt from tax. IRC § 265(a)(2).

IRC § 103(a). GI does not include interest on any State or local bonds which are used for traditional government purposes such as financing schools, roads and sewers. All other bonds are "private activity" bonds which are not exempt unless they fall within a specific exemption, or are otherwise disqualified under the statute.

Specific exemptions for "private activity" bonds include airports, docks, mass commuting facilities, hazardous waste facilities, certain electric & gas and enterprise zone facility bonds. IRC §§ 141(e)(1)(A); and 142(a)(1)-(8).

IRC § 103(b) The exclusion accorded by subsection (a) does not apply to:
   a. Bonds which do not meet the registration requirements of IRC § 149(c)
   b. Any "private activity" bonds which are not "qualified bonds" (*See* IRC § 141, *infra*).
   c. Arbitrage Bonds within the meaning of IRC § 148
   d. Industrial Revenue Bond (IRB).

* *Rationale*: Government issuer transfers its tax-exempt status to a private borrower and the federal government gives up revenues to subsidize the borrowing costs of private industry.

* Taxes are paid on interest generated by Private Activity Bonds, Arbitrage Bonds and Industrial Revenue Bonds, but, all these bonds are taxed at a lower rate.

South Carolina v. Baker, 485 U.S. 505 (1988)
IRC § 144 says if the bond is required to be registered (as most are), (almost all) then it must be registered as tax free under IRC § 103. South Carolina argued that this requirement was unconstitutional, in that they were required to issue only registered bonds.
Held: It is constitutional to deny tax exemptions on interest derived from unregistered bonds.

2. Income from United States savings bonds used to pay higher education tuition and fees: **IRC § 135.**

If a qualified US treasury bond is redeemed in order to pay tuition, and other expenses of qualified higher education, the maximum amount excludable may not exceed the excess of redemption proceeds over such qualified higher education expenses. IRC § 135(b). The interest earned is taxable to the extent that redemption proceeds exceeds the qualified expenses.

3. Private activity bond and qualified bond: IRC § 141.

    a. Private Activity Bond:
       Not tax exempt, but when taxed, the tax will be paid on income at a lower rate.

IRC § 141(a) Private Activity Bond (must pay tax on income) is any bond that is part of an issue that meets the "Private Business" Test (IRC § 141(b)(1), **and** the Private security or Payment test IRC § 141(b)(2)).

IRC § 141(b)
    i. *Private business test* -- more than 10% of proceeds are to be used for any private business use.
    ii. *Private security test* -- IRC § 141(b)(1) will **not be satisfied where payment of the principal or interest** on more than 10% of the proceeds is directly or indirectly secured by:
       * any interest in property used or to be used for a private business purpose or payments in respect of such property (IRC § 141(b)(2)(A), or

    iii. *5% Test* -- if the lesser of 5% or 5 million of the proceeds is used for any private business use not related to any governmental use, the Private Security test is modified by substituting 5% instead of 10% IRC § 141(b)(3)(A)(i))

    b. Qualified Bond: **IRC § 141(e)(1)**
(interest is not included in gross income) is a private activity bond that is tax exempt and if such bond is:

* Exempt facility bond, qualified mortgage bond, qualified veterans mortgage bond, qualified small issue bond, or a qualified student loan bond, qualified redevelopment bond, or a qualified 501(c)(3) charitable bond.

IRC § 141(e)(2) To be "qualified" within IRC § 141(e)(1) must meet the volume cap defined in IRC § 146, and

IRC § 141(e)(3) must meet tax requirements of IRC §147

4. Exempt Facility Bonds: **IRC § 142** (not included in GI under IRC § 141(e))

These are tax exempt Qualified Private Activity Bonds where 95% or more of the net proceeds of which are to be used to provide major municipal facilities with public qualities such as inter alia (among other things), private airports, docks and wharves, sewage facilities, mass communications, "qualified residential rental projects," private utilities or "qualified enhancements of hydroelectric generating facilities"

IRC § 141(d). Residential housing projects: 20% of residents must be in the "50% or less" category of area median income.
Thus, this exemption is *not limited to low income housing*.

5. Mortgage revenue bonds: **IRC § 143** (not included in GI under IRC § 141).

Requirements for exemption:
a. All proceeds are used to finance residential housing,
b. Cannot have an ownership interest in the housing for three years prior to the mortgage.

6. Qualified small issue bond: Qualified, student loan bonds, redevelopment bonds: **IRC § 144**.

Any bond under $1 million (sometimes $10,000) provided 95% (or more) of the net proceeds are to be used: a) for the acquisition, construction, etc. of depreciable land or property; or b) to redeem an outstanding prior issue, which has been issued for a qualified purpose.

7. Qualified 501(c)(3) bond: **IRC § 145.**

A "qualified 501(c)(3) bond includes any private activity bond where the net proceeds of the issue are to be owned by an organization which qualifies under IRC § 501(c)(3) or is a governmental unit, subject to $150 million limitation on bonds other than hospital bonds. Consequently, this exception is basically used by university hospitals.

8. Volume Cap: IRC § 146.

A private activity bond satisfies the "volume cap" requirements of IRC § 146, if the aggregate face amount of the private activity bonds issued do not exceed the "state ceiling" for the calendar year; that is, i.e., the greater of $50 multiplied by the population of the jurisdiction of the issuing authority or $150 million.

9. Arbitrage bond: **IRC § 148**.

Arbitrage bonds are taxable. An "arbitrage bond" is a bond whose proceeds are *reasonably expected* to be used to acquire higher yielding investments or to replace funds which were used directly or indirectly to acquire "higher yielding investments."
For this purpose, a "higher yielding investment," is any investment property, such as a security in obligation and annuity contract or any investment type property, which produces a yield which is materially higher than the yield on the issue of which it is a part. IRC § 148(b).

10. Bonds must be registered to be tax exempt: **IRC § 149**.

To be tax exempt, all bonds must be registered. **IRC § 149(a).**

11. Expenses and interest relates to tax exempt income: **IRC § 265.**

No deduction allowed for interest or indebtedness incurred.

III.   CAPITAL EXPENDITURES

A. CURRENT EXPENSE v. CAPITAL EXPENDITURE

IRC § 162(a) provides for the deduction of all the *ordinary and necessary* business expenses *paid or incurred in carrying on a trade or business* of the taxpayer.

In contrast, investments in long-term assets are treated as *expenditures.* The difference is not semantical. *Expenses* are currently deductible while *expenditures* are not.

Rule of Thumb: An investment made by the taxpayer is treated as an expenditure, rather than an expense, if it brings about the acquisition of an asset or some advantage to the taxpayer having a useful life in excess of one year (IRC § 263; Reg § 1.263(a)-1).

Expenses can be deducted immediately, capital expenditures can not.

However, some business losses must be deducted through depreciation, bad debt, etc., but they cannot be deducted immediately as an expense

Expenditures can only be recovered by way of depreciation or amortization over a period generally coinciding with the benefit to the taxpayer.

Key Concept: **Repairs are expenses; improvements** or adaptations to a new or different use are **expenditures.**
Compare Reg. § 1.162-4 with Reg. § 1.263(a)(1).

    1.   Capital expenditures: IRC § 263.

* A "capital expenditure" is a change in an asset that adds to the value or useful life of an asset or makes the asset suitable for a different use.
* No personal or consumption element involved.
* Taxpayer must capitalize all of the direct or indirect costs of producing the property IRC § 263A

    Direct Costs - materials and labor
    Interest - incurred during production period

49

Overhead - such as rent, depreciation on buildings and equipment used to produce the property

Capital expenditures are added to basis and accounted for as part of purchase price. In contrast, fully deductible repairs have no impact on basis. The deduction, in and of itself, represents a complete "recovery" of the taxpayer's investment in the repair.

IRC § 263(a)(1) Provides that a deduction shall ^not^ be allowed for any amount paid out for:
New buildings, permanent improvements or betterment's that increase the value of any property or estate. NO *current* deduction is allowable by reason of the capital expenditure. However, expenditures for tangible personal property or real property after December 31, 1980 are subject to the accelerated cost recovery system (ACRS), which was substantially modified in 1986 and is referred to as modified accelerated cost recovery system (MASRS). Even intangible property may be depreciated. The stumbling block here has always been establishing a limited period of utility, i.e., a "reasonably determinable useful life" for the intangible asset. Some assets, such as good will, are essentially not depreciable, because this period of limited utility could not be established. However, since 1987, IRC § 197 has provided that the cost of obtaining goodwill could be amortized over a period of not less than 15 years. *See also* IRC § 248 (permitting certain organizational expenditures of a corporation to be amortized over a period of not less than 60 months).

IRC § 263(a)(1) provides that the limitation regarding capital expenditures does not apply to:
* Expenditures for the development of new mines deductible under IRC § 616
* Research and experimental expenditures deductible under IRC § 174
* Soil & water conservation deductible under IRC § 175
* Expenditures by farmers for fertilizer deductible under IRC § 180
* Expenditures for removal of architectural or transportation barriers for the elderly and handicapped deductible under IRC § 190
* Expenditures for tertiary injectant is deductible under IRC § 193
* Expenditures deductible under IRC §179 (depreciable business assets).

A capital expenditure receives similar treatment to the purchase price. That is, it is reflected in basis. In fact, the rule is that the purchase price, together with all related acquisition cost, such as attorney's fees, title clearance costs, etc. must be capitalized.

Woodward v. Comm'r., 397 U.S. 572 (1972)
Costs of acquiring an asset, including all ancillary costs, must be capitalized.
Held: Buyer had to capitalize appraisal fees associated with acquisition of stock

INDOPCO v. Comm'r., 503 U.S. 79, 112 S. Ct. 1039 (1992)
Capitalization may be required even if no separate asset is acquired.
Held: Expenses incurred in takeover represented the acquisition cost of a lasting benefit and, therefore, had to be capitalized.

2.   Capitalization & inclusion in inventory costs of certain expenditures: IRC § 263A.

*   Notwithstanding its apparent breadth, IRC § 263 was considerably broadened by the introduction of IRC § 263A in 1986.
    IRC § 263A provides that a taxpayer must capitalize all of the direct or indirect costs of producing property inventory of "any other property."
*   The capitalization requirement is only applicable to property used by taxpayer in the trade or business.

§ **263A(a)** Non-deductibility of certain direct and indirect costs:
  (1) With respect to inventory in the hands of the taxpayer and "any other property", certain costs incurred in producing the inventory or property must be capitalized.
  (2) For this purpose, the term "costs" includes both direct (materials & labor) and indirect costs (such as taxes)
 (b) (1) IRC § 263A applies to real or tangible personal property produced by the taxpayer, i.e., including movies, books, music (etc.)); or
  (2) (a) Real or personal property described in IRC § 1221(1), which is acquired by the taxpayer for resale.
  (b) Only applies to taxpayers with average annual gross receipts in excess of $10,000,000.

General exceptions to the requirement:

IRC § 263A(c) is not applicable to property for taxpayer's own personal use, research and experimental expenditures for which a deduction is allowable under IRC § 174 (IRC § 263A(c)(2), developmental, and other costs of oil and gas wells and other mineral properties for which a deduction is allowable under IRC §§ 263(c), 263(i), 291(b)(2), 616 or 617(IRC § 263A(c)(3).

IRC § 263A(d) is an exception for farming business expenses that produce livestock or plants.

IRC § 263A(h) provides that free-lancers such as writers, artists and photographers are excluded with regard to their "qualified creative expenses," as that term is defined in IRC § 263A(h)(2). The term includes any trade or business expense of an individual engaged (other than as an employee) in the business of being a writer, photographer, or artist and which would otherwise be allowable as a deduction.

Example:
The cost of constructing new factory not only includes cost of bricks and concrete, but also labor cost.
Note: Ordinarily the costs of labor would be currently deductible under IRC § 162.

Note also:
As with any other cost that must be capitalized, adjustments to the taxpayer's basis in property must be made to reflect this fact. Depending on the nature of the property -- business or personal -- at least some of these costs can then be recovered either through depreciation or amortization while the asset is held or recovered upon the sale or exchange of the asset. *See* IRC §§ 167, 168, 1001.
* Must capitalize all expenditures in creating assets that will produce income.
* One cannot currently deduct an in-house expense, such as overhead, if it is producing a long-term asset:
* The direct cost of producing property, material and labor, may not be deducted if such producing property is used to create assets that will produce income. This requires capitalization of various overhead items including rent or depreciation on buildings and equipment used to produce the property.

* The cost of designing a package for a new product must be capitalized since it will benefit sales in the future, as well as currently; amortized over a five year period. IRC § 263A(a)(2)(B)
* IRC § 263A only applies to companies with sales greater than $10,000,000, therefore small businesses are exempt. IRC § 263A(b)(2)(B).
* IRC § 263A is not applicable to intangible items IRC § 263A(b)(1).
* Marketing and advertising expenses, and general administrative expenses that do not relate to the sale or production do not have to be capitalized. IRC § 263A.

3. Start-up expenditures: IRC § 195

General Rule: IRC § 195(a) "start-up expenditures" must be capitalized
Background: to be currently deductible under IRC § 162, the taxpayer must be engaged *in carrying on* a trade or business. By definition, therefore, expenses paid or incurred *prior* to the start of the business should not be currently deductible. Nonetheless, IRC § 195 provides for a limited exception under IRC § 195(b) Taxpayers may elect to amortize capitalized amounts over a period of not less than 60 months.
* If business closes before all expenditures are amortized, the unamortized amount may be deducted as a loss under IRC §165

IRC § 195 (c)(1)(A) Start-up expenditures are any amounts paid or incurred in connection with;
* Investigating the creation of trade or business, or
* Creating an active trade or business, or
* The producing of income before business begins.

IRC § 195(c)(1)(B): Amounts which, if paid in connection with an existing business, would be deductible in the year paid or incurred.

IRC § 195(d) The election to amortize must be made on or before the end of the first taxable year that the business begins. IRC § 195(d)(1).

Note*:*
* Start-up expenses do not include: expenses for interest paid or accrued on indebtedness; (IRC § 163(a)); for state and local taxes (IRC § 164); for research and experimental expenditures (IRC § 174). IRC § 195 (c)(1)
* Cost of expanding an existing business is treated as an expense of such business, except to the extent it is allocable to capitalized assets.

B. DEPRECIATION

Purpose: Notwithstanding the rules regarding capitalization IRC § 167(a) permits ". . . a reasonable allowance for the *exhaustion, wear and tear,* including a reasonable allowance for *obsolescence* , of:
* property used in the trade or business, or
* property held for the production of income."

   1. Depreciation: IRC § 167

IRC § 167(a) Depreciation deduction is allowed for the exhaustion, and wear and tear (including obsolescence) of:
* Tangible property used in trade or business, or held for the production of income (Cost of land, securities or property not used in connection with a trade or business of the taxpayer or an income productive activity of the taxpayer may neither be depreciated nor amortized).

IRC § 167(c) provides that the measure of depreciation is determined in part by the taxpayer's basis in the asset. That is, the unadjusted basis of the asset *plus* subsequent capitalized expenditures related to the asset *minus* the amount of depreciation *previously allowed or allowable.* Where no method of depreciation has been chosen by the taxpayer, the depreciation imputed -- the amount *allowable* -- is measured by the straight-line method.

   2. Limitations on Depreciation
      a. Passive Loss Rules: deductions related to passive activities can't exceed income from those activities (IRC § 469)
      b. At Risk Limitation: (IRC § 465) depreciation can't exceed the amount of the taxpayer's actual investment and personal liability obligation

    c.   Property worth less than the debt: If property is worth less than the net personal liability, the taxpayer cannot deduct. *Estate of Franklin v. Comm'r*; and *Pleasant Summit Land Corp. v. Comm'r.*,

    d.   Activities *not* engaged in For Profit: *See* IRC § 183.

Note: Intangible property must be amortized, not depreciated. (See IRC § 197).

3.   Depreciation Schedule

To accurately construct a schedule of depreciation, taxpayer must know:
    a.   Basis (use adjusted basis under IRC §1011)
    b.   Method of depreciation under IRC §168(a)(2);
    c.   Convention (when placed in service during the taxable year) under IRC §168(a)(3);
    d.   Salvage value (IRC § 168(b)(4) treats the salvage value of property under the accelerated cost recovery system (ACRS) as zero). For tangible property, a "reasonable allowance" is permitted under IRC § 167;
    e.   Recovery period under IRC §168(a)(1) and (c)

Note: where IRC § 168 does not apply, depreciation is ordinarily calculated on the "useful life" of the asset in the taxpayer's trade or business or income producing activities.

Where the taxpayer is subject to an alternative minimum tax (AMT) calculation under IRC § 55 and has taken depreciation deductions in computing regular tax liability, the taxpayer's alternative minimum taxable income in general is computed by using longer depreciation periods. This produces lower deductions and a higher AMT. In some cases, the 1997 Act liberalizes the AMT provisions in favor of the taxpayer in industries that have intensive demands on capital and for certain "small business corporations."

4.   Accelerated cost recovery system (ACRS): IRC § 168.

IRC § 168(a) Depreciation under IRC § 167 is determined using the applicable: (i) depreciation method, (ii) recovery period and (iii) convention.
If an election to use the straight line method is made, it applies to all property in that class and is irrevocable. IRC § 168(b)(5).

*   The Accelerated Cost Recovery System (ACRS) front loads
       depreciation to get the tax benefit in the early years.
*   The ACRS is not applicable to intangible property, (i.e., goodwill).

    a.   Applicable depreciation methods: IRC § 168(b)(1).

        i. Switching from Double Declining Method to Straight Line
       Method
       IRC § 168(b)(1)(A) General Rule: Unless the taxpayer
       elects otherwise, the double declining balance method switches
       to the straight line method.

        ii. Switching to Straight line Method
       IRC § 168(b)(1)(B) Switching to straight line method for
       the first taxable year for which using the straight-line method
       will yield a higher depreciation allowance (generally applicable).

        iii. Declining Balance to Straight Line Method
       IRC § 168(b)(2) 150% declining balance method (with a
       switch to the straight line method) is used only in specific
       circumstances that is when:
           a)   property is "15-year" or "20-year" property,
           b)   property is used in the business of farming; or
           c)   if taxpayer elects to do so.

        iv. Straight line Method
       IRC § 168(b)(3) Straight Line Method applies to:
           a)   nonresidential real property,
           b)   residential rental property,
           c)   railroad grading or tunnel bore, any property classified
              under IRC § 168(e)(3)(D)(ii) (still any tree or vine
              bearing fruit or nuts).
Straight-line depreciation involves allocating the cost of an
asset over the number of years in its recovery.

For this purpose "cost" is the unadjusted basis of the asset plus
subsequent capitalized expenditures related to the asset.

IRC § 168(b)(4) Salvage value is treated as zero using
ACRS.

b.   Applicable Recovery Period: **IRC § 168(b)(1).**

IRC § 168(c) Applicable Recovery Period

*   depends on the type (classification) of property -- refer to chart in IRC § 168(e)
*   for property placed in service prior to 1981, salvage value was taken into account and the recovery was determined by the estimated useful life of the asset. These concepts are now relevant only when IRC § 168 is inapplicable.

c.   Applicable convention: **IRC § 168(d).**

*   Generally, property is deemed to have been purchased and sold half-way through the year (Mid-year convention)(means only one-half year's depreciation is allowed in the year in which the asset is placed in service and in the year in which the asset is disposed of)
*   Nonresidential real property, residential rental property and RR grading or tunnel bore uses the mid-month convention (i.e., asset is deemed to have been placed in service at the midpoint of the last quarter)
*   If substantial property has been placed in service during the last three months of the year then mid-quarter method is used (placed into service in the midpoint of the quarter).

Example:

Taxpayer purchases "qualified technological equipment" within IRC § 168(e)(3)(D)(iv) for $10,000. The equipment, which is exclusively used in the taxpayer's trade or business, qualifies as five year depreciable property under IRC § 168(e)(3)(B). However, the recovery period will extend into the sixth year. This is due to the "applicable half year convention" explained in the example *infra*.

The straight line depreciation *with applicable mid-year convention* will be calculated as follows:

Straight Line with applicable Mid-Year Convention

Year	Depreciable Basis	%	Depreciation Allowance
1	10,000	10%	1,000*
2	10,000	20%	2,000
3	10,000	20%	2,000
4	10,000	20%	2,000
5	10,000	20%	2,000
6	10,000	10%	1,000*

* applicable Mid-Year convention.
* The availability of pre-computed percentages substantially simplify the process of calculating the annual allowance. Rev. Proc. 87-57, 1987-2 C.B.687.
The above example does not reflect the impact of an election under IRC § 179. *See* discussion *infra*.

d. Classification of Property
IRC § 168(e) Provides for the classification of a specific type of property. This classification determines the applicable recovery period for the asset. There are six categories, which are based on "class life":

   i.   **IRC §168(e)(2)** Classifies real property as either residential (27.5 year recovery period) or nonresidential (39 year recovery period) real property.

   ii.   **IRC §168(b)(3)** Implications of method and convention: straight line (slower) for real estate

   iii. **IRC §168(d)(2)** Mid-month convention, not mid-year Property to which IRC § 168 does not apply:
* film and videotape, sound recordings (IRC §§ 168(f)(3) and 168(f)(4))
* public utility property (IRC § 168(f)(2))
* property placed, in a service in a churning transaction
* property for which the taxpayer elects to use the "unit-of-production method" (IRC § 168(f)(1)).

e.   Double Declining Balance.

Double Declining Balance 100% (useful x 2) x Basis

* Before IRC § 168 was enacted, the maximum depreciation allowance to which a taxpayer was entitled would ordinarily be computed under the double declining balance method of depreciation. In capsule, double declining balance (DBB) computes depreciation by applying a percentage, which is twice that of the straight line rate, to the taxpayer's basis in the property, which declines to reflect previous depreciation allowed or allowable.

* An important feature of DBB is appreciation is that while it produces substantially larger deductions in the early years of an asset's useful life, the drop off is sharp and ultimately lower than straight line. It is for this reason that the mandated methods under IRC § 168 start out with double declining balance and switch to straight line to maintain higher deductions for the taxpayer.

* Can double straight line percentage in first year of asset's useful life?

* Year two uses the same percentage but is applied to the new balance (initial basis *plus* post acquisition capital improvements *less* previous depreciation). *Note:* Because the percentage for depreciation is applied against a shrinking basis, at some point inevitably -- declining balance depreciation will produce *less than* straight-line)

Example:
Taxpayer acquires equipment for use in his trade or business. The equipment, which costs $100,000, has a reasonably estimated useful life of 10 years. As a result, the correct recovery period is 7 years under IRC § 168(c). The interaction of the double declining balance (200% DB) method of depreciation with a switch to straight line can be illustrated as follows:

Depreciable Year	Basis	%	Depreciation Allowance
1	100,000	14.29%	14,290
2	100,000	24.49%	24,490
3	100,000	17.49%	17,490
4	100,000	12.49%	12,490
5	100,000	8.93%**	8,930
6	100,000	8.93%	8,930
7	100,000	4.46%	4,460

**Switch to Straight Line as directed by IRC 168(b)(1)(A) and (B)

Rev. Proc. 87-57, 1987-2 C.B. 687 provides pre-computed percentages, which substantially simplifies the process of calculating the annual allowance.
Example does not reflect the impact of an election under IRC § 179. *See* discussion *infra.*

Simon v. Comm'r., 68 F. 3d 41 (2d Cir.1995).
A musician bought 19th century bows. As they were used, they decreased in value as musical instruments but increased in value as antiques.

Held: That the bows would suffer exhaustion, wear and tear as musical instruments and thus could be depreciated, even though as antiques and works of art they would not suffer such "wear and tear". As artwork, they do not suffer wear and tear.
This is an issue of timing and, perhaps, a change in the character of the gain ultimately to be realized by the taxpayer musician upon the sale, exchange, or other disposition of the bows because musician will be taxed on the gain at the time of sale. *See* discussion of "depreciation recapture," *infra.*

5. Election to expense certain depreciable assets: **IRC § 179.**

Taxpayers who purchase tangible personal property for use in their trade or business may elect to "expense", i.e., immediately deduct up to $17,500 of the cost of such assets. Any amount deducted under this elective provision is not subject to depreciation (taxpayer can't recover cost twice). For every dollar of qualified section 179 property placed in service during the taxable year in excess of $200,00, the limitation on the election is reduced by $1. Consequently, if the taxpayer invests $217,500 in IRC § 179 property this elective option will be essentially foreclosed.

When a IRC § 179 election is made the taxpayer's basis in the asset must be reduced (100,000 - 17,500 = 82,500) (IRC § 1016 basis), then start depreciation.

   a. "Recapture" of Depreciation
   Special provisions require the taxpayer to report as ordinary income, not capital gain, certain portions of any gain attributable to prior depreciation. Also, recapture amounts do not qualify for deferral under the installment method.
      i.   *Personal property* : IRC § 1245 provides that recognized gain on depreciation of personal property is treated as ordinary income to the extent gain it is attributable to depreciation;
      ii. *Real Property:* General rule is that depreciation is "recaptured," i.e., treated as ordinary income rather than capital gain, only if accelerated depreciation (that is, measured by the excess of depreciation actually allowed over what would have been allowed under straight-line depreciation) was taken.
   *   All tangible personal property (i.e., machinery) IRC § 1245(a)
   *   Recomputed Bases = adjusted basis + depreciation
   Amounts deducted in the year purchased under § 179 also should be added. The amount by which the lower of the recomputed basis or amount realized exceeds the adjusted basis is treated as ordinary income

Example 1:
Taxpayer acquires a car for $25,000 for exclusive use in his trade or business. After depreciation of $18,000 has been taken, the taxpayer sells the car for $11,000. Taxpayer's gain realized is $4,000 (the amount for which the car was sold equals $11,000.

Basis in the car was $7,000 ($25,000 minus $18,000 = $7,000)). Then, the entire $4,000 of gain realized will be characterized as ordinary income, rather than capital gain, The rule is that the lower of the **excess of:** (i) "**recomputed basis**" ($7,000 plus $18,000 of depreciation deductions = $25,000) *over* the taxpayer's **adjusted basis;** or (ii) the **amount realized** ($11,000) upon the sale, etc. over the taxpayer's **basis** for which the depreciable asset was sold is to be treated as ordinary income. Here, since the asset actually declined in value, *all* the gain is attributable to depreciation. In other words, the only reason there is any gain is due to the fact that the taxpayer's basis declined.

Example 2:
If the car and the previous example were sold for $28,000, the taxpayer's gain would be $21,000 ($28,000 minus $7,000 = $21,000). However, only $18,000 of the gain would be characterized as ordinary income due to depreciation recapture. The remaining $3,000 would be treated as Section 1231 (capital) gain.

6.   Amortization of goodwill and other intangibles: IRC § 197.
A taxpayer can deduct the amortization of any intangible property listed in this section. Use the adjusted basis for this computation with the Straight Line Method & 15 years even if its useful life is less than 15 years. No other depreciation or amortization of an IRC § 197 intangible is allowed.

IRC § 197 An intangible property is amortizable:
   a.   when it is acquired by the taxpayer after enactment and held for trade or business IRC § 212; and
   b.   if it is an intangible that is NOT created by the taxpayer. The following are IRC § 197 amortizable intangibles: Goodwill, Going Concern Value; Work Force in Place, Business Books, Records, Operating Systems, Information Systems--Lists, Patent, Copyright, Formula, Process, Design, Pattern, Format, Know How, Customer Base Intangible (Market Share, Relationships), Supplier Base Intangible (Relationships), License permits, other rights granted by the government, covenant not to compete entered into upon an acquisition, franchise, trademark or trade name.

Exceptions:
* The following IRC § 197 Intangibles are **not** amortizable:
    ⇒ Interest in a partnership, trust or estate
    ⇒ Stock Interest
    ⇒ Any interest in Land
    ⇒ Interests under lease agreements
    ⇒ Franchise rights for a professional sport team
    ⇒ Computer software available for purchase throughout the US or, that is not acquired in an acquisition of assets
    ⇒ Acquired interest in film, sound, book... patent, or copyright, and rights to receive such intangible property under a contract are
    ⇒ not amortizable unless they are acquired in the purchase of a business or trade, not when created.

Newark Star Morning Ledger Co. v. U.S., 507 U.S. 546, 113 S. Ct. 1670 (1993)
Purchased a newspaper, allocated $67.8 million to "paid subscribers". This was for all of the pre-purchased subscriptions. Government said that this was nondepreciable.
Held: Since they could establish a determinable useful life, the value of the assets could be amortized.
IRC § 197 imposes a 15 year amortization period regardless of the circumstances.

Note:
* Depreciate intangibles over 15 years even if the useful life is less than 15 years
* Patents or copyrights may last longer
* Goodwill = expectation of continued patronage

Tax Planning: Since land is not deductible, if one buys land with a building on it, one allocates more of the cost to the building.

IV. DEDUCTIONS, EXPENSES AND LOSSES

IRC § 1(e) imposes a tax on the Taxable Income of various categories of individual taxpayers including trust and estates. *The difference between an individual's Gross Income and Taxable Income is deductions.* Taxable Income deductions are classified as either "above-the-line" or "below-the-line". The latter category is sometimes referred to as "itemized" deductions. The distinction is important, because itemized deductions must be balanced against the taxpayer's standard deduction. The taxpayer is entitled to take whichever yields a larger deduction and a lower tax bracket. In contrast, "above-the-line" deductions, i.e., business deductions in general, maybe taken *in **addition*** to the taxpayer's itemized deductions or standard deductions, as the case may be.

When the taxpayer is an individual, there are substantial limitations on deductions. For taxpayers who are not engaged in a specific trade or business, most deductions will be classified as "personal" and, therefore, not deductible at all. IRC § 262. However, various exceptions exist for income-producing activities, the maintenance of income-producing property or tax advice (IRC § 212), interest paid subject to limitations (IRC § 163), taxes, including state property and income taxes (IRC § 164), losses (IRC § 165), etc.

Although this Chapter is devoted to deductions, it must be understood that not all expenses, even those incurred in carrying on a trade or business of the taxpayer, are *currently* deductible. These include investments in certain long-term assets, i.e., those from which the taxpayer anticipates a benefit substantially beyond the taxable year. Such expenditures are classified as capital expenditures and the taxpayer can recover his/her/its investment only by way of depreciation or by way of reduced gain or increased loss upon the disposition of the asset.

A. BUSINESS: LOSSES, EXPENSES AND DEDUCTIONS

IRC § 162(a)Allows the various expenses of conducting a business to be deducted. Provides that "all the **ordinary and necessary** expenses **paid or incurred** in carrying on a **trade or business**" are deductible. The statute is deceptively simple.

"Necessary" does not refer to only essential business expenses. In fact, the threshold test is quite low; taxpayer's reasonable business judgment won't be questioned. (See Welch v. Herlvering, 290 U.S. 111 (1933)).

"Ordinary" refers to items that are currently deductible, rather than capital expenditures. IRC § 162(a) in general states that reasonable and necessary expenses in carrying on a trade or business are deductible.

1. Trade or business expenses: IRC § 162

    The **ordinary and necessary** business expenses **paid or incurred** during the year in the carrying on trade or business are deductible (taxpayer must be already engaged in carrying on a trade or business at the time the expense is paid or incurred; (See IRC § 195 re: "start-up" expenses). The criteria:
    a. paid in connection with taxpayer's business
    b. not personal
    c. current expense, not capital
    d. expense must be ordinary and necessary
    e. not violate public policy

Ordinary and necessary business expenses include:

* Reasonable allowance for salaries; whether a salary is "reasonable" is usually a question a fact; see Reg. §§ 1.162-7-8-9; IRC § 162(m) imposes a limitation on deductions for the most highly paid CEO's in public companies receiving salaries in excess of $1 million. Not applicable to performance based employment. Traveling expenses (including meals and lodging other than those which are lavish or extravagant) while away from home in pursuit of business, for food and beverage, only 50% of cost is deductible (IRC § 274(n))

* Rentals or other payments to be made as a condition to the continued use or possession, for the purpose of the trade or business, of property in which the taxpayer has not taken title or in which he has no equity. IRC § 162(a)(3).
* A member of Congress resides in the district which she represents, but she can only deduct yearly living expenses up to $3,000. The period away from home will be treated as if in pursuit of a trade or business.
* Illegal trade or business. IRC § 162 does not distinguish between legal or non-legal businesses; but see IRC § 162(c) regarding bribes to government and nongovernment officials and (f) relating to fines or penalties imposed by government for the violation of any law.
* Expenses for illegal activities that are not in themselves inherently illegal are deductible; see U. S. v. Sullivan 356 U.S. 27 (1958)

Trade or Business Expenses Not Deductible Under IRC § 162:

* If the amount is deductible as a charitable contribution, then it is not deductible as a business expense. IRC § 162(b).
* Illegal Bribes, Kickbacks, and other payments. IRC § 162(c).
* Illegal payments to government officials. IRC § 162(c).
* Any fine or penalty paid to a government for a violation of any law. IRC § 162(f).
* Two-thirds of damages for antitrust violations are not deductible. IRC § 162(g).
* Certain lobbying and political expenditures.
* Influencing legislatures (not applicable to local legislature). IRC § 162(e)1(a).
* Participation in a political campaign, IRC § 162(e)(1)(b).
* Any attempt to influence the general public, IRC § 162(e)(1)(c).
* No deduction for payment of dues to a tax exempt organization. IRC § 162(e)(3).

Exceptions:
* If it is a local governing organization then can deduct money expended to appear before it. IRC § 162(e)(2).
* De minimis provision for in-house expenditures up to $ 2,000. IRC § 162(e)(5)(B).
* Lobbyist can deduct non-reimbursed trade and business expenses. IRC § 162(e)(5)(C).

Note:
* Attorney's fees incurred in fighting criminal sanctions may be deductible, provided paid or incurred in connection with the conduct of the taxpayer's trade or business; (see Comm'r. v. Tellier, 383 U.S. 687 (1966) (taxpayer able to deduct attorney's fee, even though he was convicted of securities fraud; allegation and defense were "ordinary and necessary" in the taxpayer's trade or business, and attorney's fees and legal expenses are customary in the business world).
* Traveling to and from work, i.e., commuting, is not deductible because it is a matter of personal choice of and for the convenience of the taxpayer (Flowers v. Comm'r., 326 U.S. 465 (1946)).
* Trips between several businesses may be deductible. Also, trips between home and temporary work locations, if Taxpayer has regular place of business, are deductible.
* Combined business and pleasure trips are deductible if primarily for business. In such a case, the taxpayer must allocate meals and lodging between the two.
* "Sleep or Rest" Rule - meals are only deductible when taxpayer is away from home on an overnight trip or at least for a period which requires "sleep or rest"
* Temporary v. Indefinite: Taxpayer can deduct cost of 2nd temporary home if employment ties taxpayer to both places. To deduct expenses at a temporary location, there must be a business reason for also maintaining home at permanent location, so that this not merely a matter of personal convenience.(Hantzis v. Comm'r. , 638 F.2d 248 (1st Cir), *cert. den'd.*, 452 U.S. 962 (1981).

Temporary Rule:
* TP needs a business connection to both cities to justify having two homes and deducting both
* If employer temporarily assigns TP to another area, then TP can deduct food, transportation and lodging without uprooting his family
* If it is used over a year, it is not considered a temporary home, it is merely indefinite. The result is that living expenses revert to nondeductible, personal expenses. See IRC § 262.
* IRC § 217 deduction for moving expenses if job adds at least 35 miles to commute.

Encyclopedia Britannica v. Comm'r., 685 F. 2d 212 (7th Cir. 1982).
Publisher attempted to deduct the cost of purchasing a manuscript
Held: not currently deductible but had to be capitalized. Expenditures made with the intent to generate income over a period of years are capital expenditures even if the manuscript was made "in house", it would still be treated as a capital asset under IRC § 263(a).

Contra, Midland, infra.

Midland Empire Packing Company v. Comm'r., 14 T.C. 635 (1950).
Company put in a concrete lining in the basement to protect it from oil spills. This was necessary, to continue using the basement for storage of meat, and although a one time expenditure, it was also ordinary.
Held; This was a repair, therefore deductible. A repair merely serving to keep property in an operating condition for the purpose for which it was used is an ordinary expense.

* Ordinary does not mean habitual, but rather the expense would be common and is an accepted means of combating the problem.
* Repairs are usually expenses, but if they make the property more valuable, extend useful life, or convert the property to a new or different use, it is now a capital improvement
* Repairs, in contrast to replacements, are currently deductible expenses; compare Reg. §§1.162-4 and 1.263(a)-1(a).\

Reg. § 1.263(a)-(2) illustrates various "capital expenditures", which include the cost of acquisition, construction or erection of buildings machinery and equipment, etc; cost of securing copyright to property or in clearing titled property; architects fees; and commissions paid in purchasing securities.

Rule:
All expenditures which create assets that will produce future income must be capitalized.

Definitions:

Trade or Business is not specifically defined in IRC. *See Comm'r. v. Groetzinger* 480 U.S. 23 (1987)

* Activity entered into with the expectation of making a profit;
* Regularity and continuity in the operation of the activity;
* Taxpayer must be actively engaged in pursuing it (either himself or through agents).

Ordinary & Necessary

* Ordinary--expenses must relate to transactions of common or frequent occurrence in that type of business (*Deputy v. Dupont*, 51 T.C.M. 515 (1966))
* Necessary--imposes only the minimal requirement that the expense be appropriate and helpful for the business (*Welch v. Helvering*, 290 U.S. 111 (1993))

Note: *Factors to look for*:

* Is the expense voluntary or legally obligated?
* If it is a common payment, then it is usually deductible?
* Just because it is a one time occurrence (heavy litigation fees) does not obviate the ordinary and necessary status of an expense?
* Is the cost of services reasonable?

Gilliam v. Comm'r., 51 T.C.M. 515 (1986)

Artist on a business trip took an anti-depressant. He became violent and attacked a passenger on the plane. Artist deducted legal expenses incurred as a business expense.

Held: This was not an ordinary business expense, but rather an extraordinary expense. He was not carrying out trade or business and not helping to produce more income.

INDOPCO v. Comm'r., 112 S. CT. 1039 (1992)

Investment banking and legal expenses incurred during a friendly takeovers were not deductible--must be capitalized.

Held: Court rejected the notion that an outlay had to produce some specific asset in order to be capitalized.

* There is no deduction for education to meet the minimum requirements in a person's field, or to teach a person a new trade or business, e.g., law school. However, if the taxpayer is already qualified to practice in his/her field, education is deductible in two situations:

a. maintains or improves skills *required by the job* (above the expected *minimum* requirement)
b. courses required by law or the employer as a condition to maintain the job, status or rate of compensation.

Carroll v. Comm'r., 418 F.2d 91 (7th Cir. 1969)
Deductions are not allowed for education expenses which are not related to or required by the taxpayer's job.

2. Goodwill.

Goodwill may be deducted as an ordinary business expense if it is used to repair or retain already existing goodwill. However, if the purpose is to acquire new goodwill, the cost must be amortized under IRC § 197.

Reasonable Goodwill Costs = Expense

Purchase to acquire new Goodwill = Capital Expenditure

Welch v. Helvering, 290 U.S. 111 (1933)
Welch paid off debts of defunct company to solidify credit with suppliers without any obligation to do so.
Held: This was a capital expenditure rather than a business expense since he was in effect purchasing goodwill even though this expense may have been necessary to the success of the business, paying someone else's debts is not ordinary.
An outlay for the development of a new reputation and goodwill is a capital expenditure

M.L. Eakes v. Comm'r., 686 F. 2d 217 (4th Cir. 1982)
Current deductions were allowed for payments of the debts of a predecessor corporation that was insolvent. There is nothing unusual about repaying debts to establish credit and preserve an existing business (rather than building a new one).

3. Expenses for production of income: **IRC § 212.**
    (Subject to 2% floor limitation re: "Miscellaneous Itemized Deductions")

The expense must be a current outlay, "ordinary and necessary, not violative of public policy and incurred for the production or management of income producing property". IRC § 212 provides:
In the case of an individual, there shall be allowed as a deduction all ordinary and necessary expenses paid or incurred in the taxable year for:
  a. production or collection of income,
  b. management, conservation, or maintenance for property held in the production of income, or
  c. in connection with the determination, collection and refund of any tax

Note:
IRC § 212 expenses (other than rent and royalties) are deducted from AGI below-the-line, and are subject to the rule that allows deduction of miscellaneous itemized deductions only in excess. See IRC §§ 67 (a) and (b); and 62(a)(4).

4. Disallowance of certain expenses in connection with business use of home, rental of vacation homes and others : **IRC § 280A.**

*   Generally, a home office is not deductible

IRC § 280A(a)   No deduction is allowed for a dwelling unit that is used by the taxpayer as a residence (except as otherwise provided).

IRC § 280A(b)   Deduction is allowable in connection with a trade or business or income producing activity

IRC § 280A(c)(1) When dwelling is exclusively used on a regular basis as:
(**A**) The principal place of business for any trade or business of the taxpayer
(**B**) The place of business which is used by patients, clients, or customers in meeting or dealing with the taxpayer in the normal course of his trade or business
(**C**) A separate structure (garage) not attached to the dwelling unit in connection with the

taxpayer's trade or business is not deductible if it is rented to an employer. Employees are permitted to deduct "home office" expenses incurred in connection with the employers trade or business and which are "for the convenience of" the taxpayer's employer.

IRC § 280A(c)(2) Deduction is allowable for use of the dwelling unit as storage space as long as this is the sole fixed location of such a trade or business.

IRC § 280A(c)(3) Deduction is allowed for expenses attributed to parts that are rented.

IRC § 280A(c)(4) **(A)** Deduction is allowed for a portion of a dwelling unit used as a day-care facility for children or elders, or mentally handicapped.
(B) Only if the operator is licensed, applied for one or is exempt.
(C) Amount deductible is in the same proportion as the amount of time that it is used as a Day-Care facility bears to the total time it is available for use.

IRC § 280A(c)(5) Limitation on deduction.
The aggregate deductions allowable *shall not exceed the excess of the GI derived from the use* over the sum of the deductions allocable to the trade or activity plus the deductions allowed whether or not the dwelling unit was so utilized.

IRC § 280A(d)(1) Limitation on the deduction applies only if the dwelling unit is used *as a residence,* i.e., for personal purposes for a number of days which exceeds the greater of 14 days or 10% of the number of days during the year that the unit is rented.

IRC § 280A(d)(2) Personal purposes = if any part of a day, a taxpayer or family member uses the residence, or if any individual uses the residence under an arrangement with the taxpayer where taxpayer still uses a portion (whether or not rent is paid), the days count as personal days.

IRC § 280A(d)(3) Rental to family members as long as the FMV rent is paid is not a personal day. A dwelling unit is a house, apartment, boat, condo, mobile home, etc.

* A dwelling unit does not include the portion of a unit used as a motel, hotel or inn.

IRC § 280A(g) Special rule for certain rental use
If the taxpayer resides in the dwelling unit and rents it for less than 15 days, then no deductions whether under IRC §280A or IRC § 183, are allowable. Moreover, any income derived from such use will not be included in the taxpayer's gross income under IRC § 61.

Moller v. U.S., 721 F. 2d 810 (Fed Cir.1983), *cert. den'd.* 467 U.S. 1251 (1984)
Taxpayers were retired with an investment portfolio. They spent their time managing their money. They attempted to deduct the cost of a home office
Held: No deduction under § 280A, since they were not engaged in a trade or business. They were investors, not traders.
Had they rented an office, there would have been no problem since under IRC § 212 they would be engaged in a profit making business.

Comm'r. v. Soliman, 506 U.S. 168 (1983).
Anesthesiologist attempted to deduct the expenses of a home office.
He only worked there for a few hours making calls and keeping records, etc. His principal place of business was the hospital.
Held: There needs to be a high threshold to allow an individual to deduct a home office
Two prong test to determine principal place of business is used:
    a.   the relative importance of the functions performed at each business; and
    b.   the amount of time spent at a home location

Note:
* If one has more than one place of business, one must determine which one is principal.
* If one is an employee, one must prove that the use of her residence is for the convenience of the employer. That is, for example, no space is provided at work for necessary tasks.
* Vacation Homes. One can still deduct taxes, and casualty losses, however :

* If used as a residence under IRC § 280A for more than 14 days or 10% of the number of rental days during the year, then one can't deduct items "not otherwise allowable. That is, there can be no deduction for items such as depreciation, which are not otherwise allowable and which require a "trade or business" or "income-productive" activity nexus means in order to qualify for deduction.
* If one uses it for personal purposes (including some rental), only that portion properly allocable to rental is deductible.

5. Expenditures in connection with the illegal sale of drugs: **IRC § 280E.**

* No deduction or credit allowed for any expenses incurred in the taxable year due to the trafficking of a controlled substance which is prohibited under Federal Law.

B. PERSONAL LOSSES, EXPENSES AND DEDUCTIONS

1. Losses

    a. Losses Defined: **IRC § 165**.

    IRC § 165 Losses

    * Deduction allowed for any loss sustained and not compensated for by insurance or otherwise.

    * The taxpayer must file the loss with the insurance company, if applicable, in order to receive the deduction; IRC § 165(h)(4)(B), which requires that a claim be filed where a casualty loss is "covered" by insurance.

    * The basis for determining the amount of the deduction is the adjusted basis under IRC § 1011 for determining the loss from the sale, exchange or disposition of the property.

    Loss = Adjusted Basis - Amount Realized (sale price)

b.   Limitations on Losses: **IRC § 165**.

IRC § 165(c) In the case of an individual, losses are limited to:

IRC § 165(c)(1) losses in connection with trade or business (IRC § 162).

IRC § 165(c)(2) losses incurred in any transaction entered into for profit (not trade or business), (compare IRC § 212).

IRC § 165(c)(3) The measure of a casualty loss from fire, storm, shipwreck, casualty or theft greater than $100 is the lesser of the taxpayer's economic loss (the difference in fair market value of the damaged property before and after the casualty) and the taxpayer's adjusted basis in the property under IRC § 1011.
TP may only deduct to extent that loss exceeds 10% of AGI. (IRC § 165(h)(2)).

IRC § 165(d) losses from gambling are deductible only to the extent of the gains from gambling.

IRC § 165(e) losses from theft are treated as a loss sustained during the year discovered.

IRC § 165(f) Capital loss: losses from sale or exchange of capital assets are only deductible to the extent permitted by IRC § 1211 and § 1212

IRC § 165(g)(1) If any security which is a capital asset becomes worthless during the taxable year, the loss is treated as if it were from a sale or exchange of that security on the last day of the capital year.

IRC § 165(g)(2) Security = stock, right to receive stock, registered government or corporate bond

Note:
*   A loss occurs if the taxpayer has not recovered her basis at the end of the transaction
*   Personal losses are not deductible
*   If a deduction for a loss is taken, then the expense to repair the property to its pre-loss condition is not deductible. It is added to the basis.

* Amount deductible: if loss qualifies as a casualty loss, a taxpayer can deduct the lesser of:
  i.   The adjusted basis of the property, or
  ii. The difference between the value of the property before and after (reduced by $100 if it is a casualty loss)
* Taxpayer can only deduct the loss to his own property
* Suddenness requirement: Deductions in the case of an individual that are not specifically listed above in IRC § 165 (c) are only deductible if there is a sudden "casualty," which requires a sudden onset, such as a "fire, storm, shipwreck, or other casualty."
* Termite damage does not meet the suddenness requirement. *Austra v. Comm'r.,* 25 TCM78 (1966) (slow occurrence).
* If a ring is lost when a hand slams in the door, that is sudden. *White v. Comm'r.,* 48 TC430 (1967).

Dyer v. Comm'r., 20 T.C.M. 705 (1961).
One of two matching vases is broken by a family pet not covered by insurance.
Held: Denied a deduction---not a casualty (must be reasonable)

Blackman v. Comm'r., 88 T.C. 677 (1987).
Husband sets wife's clothes on fire and as a result burns down the house. Insurance would not cover the claim.
Held: Disallowed casualty deduction for losses sustained through grossly negligent conduct. Apparently, merely negligent conduct, however, will not bar deduction.

When is protection against loss deductible?

Some examples:
* Microfilming a set of back issues as a protection against destruction is a deductible expense. The business still operates on the same scale. No improvement is made. *Times v. Mirror,* 231 F.2d 876 (9th Cir. 1956)
* Drainage system installed under the threat of litigation must be capitalized. The need was foreseeable and a necessary part of the capital investment. *Morris v. Comm'r,* 25 T.C. 272 (1956).
* Required installation of a sprinkler system was capitalized. Although mandatory, it was an improvement and a permanent addition. The benefit lasted beyond the taxable *year (Hotel Sulgrave v. Comm'r,* 21 T.C. 619 (1954)).

c.   Loss from wash sales of stock or securities: **IRC § 1091**.

IRC § 1091 provides that losses from "wash sales" are not deductible. A "wash sale" involves a sale and a purchase (or a purchase and a sale within a period of 30 days of "substantially identical stock or securities.") Thus, where a taxpayer sells stock and buys it back within a period of 30 days or substitutes "substantially identical" assets within the 30 day period, the transaction is treated as a nullity and the "realized loss" is ignored. The repurchased stock retains the same basis as the original stock (increased or decreased if the repurchase price was more or less than the sale price).
IRC § 1091 and IRC § 267 disallow loss deductions on certain sales between related taxpayers (IRC § 267 defines family members).

d.   Passive activity losses and credits limited: **IRC § 469**.

Losses from passive investments are only deductible to offset income from other passive activities. Thus, if a taxpayer does not have any passive income, TP must wait to use the losses until he/she does.
Taxpayer cannot use depreciation deductions from passive activity, except as provided.
IRC § 469 was adopted to shut down tax-shelters. *See* Chapter XIII, Tax Shelters, *infra*.

Passive activity = one in which the taxpayer does not materially participate. IRC § 469(c)(1)

Materiality test: TP materially participates if they meet any of the following:
*   Spends more than 500 hours per year on the activity
*   Performs substantially all of the activities performed by all of the individuals.
*   Spends more than 100 hours, if it exceeds that of any other individual's participation.
*   Combined participation exceeds 500 hours.
*   Materially participated in the activity for any five of the last ten years
*   Materially participated in a personal service activity in any of the three prior years.

2. Personal Expenses.

    a. Medical, dental and other expenses: **IRC § 213**.

IRC § 213(a) Medical expenses for self, spouse & dependents which are not covered for by insurance but paid by taxpayer are deductible to the extent they exceed 7.5% of AGI. (This floor effectively disallows deductions for all but the most expensive medical treatment).

Perhaps significantly, IRC § 213 (a) uses the term "compensated for" by insurance. There is no parallel provision to that in IRC § 165 (h)(3)(E), which requires that a claim of loss be filed on behalf of the taxpayer who seeks a casualty loss deduction. As a practical matter, it would seem that most medical claims are routine and part of the billing procedure of the medical services provider.

IRC § 213(b) Deduction is only applicable to medicine or drugs if they are a prescribed drug or insulin.

IRC § 213(d)(1) Medical care = money actually expended and not reimbursed
*   For diagnosis, cure, mitigation, treatment or prevention of diseases, or for the purpose of affecting any structure or function of the body; or
*   For transportation primarily for and essential to medical care; or
*   For insurance including premiums paid under SS act relating to supplementary care.

IRC § 213(d)(2) Lodging while away from home is included in determining cost of medical care (up to $50/ person /night) if primarily for and essential to medical care, and if it is provided by a licensed physician without any significant element of personal pleasure, recreation or vacation.

IRC § 213(d)(9) Cosmetic Surgery (directed at improving the patients appearance but not meaningfully promoting proper functioning of the body or preventing or treating an illness or disease) not included in scope of "medical care" unless surgery is necessary to ameliorate a deformity, arising from or directly related to a congenital abnormality, disfiguring disease or a personal injury resulting from an accident or trauma.

Note:
* Insurance premiums included in 7.5% threshold.
* The costs for Braille books and magazines are deductible medical expenses.
* Legal fees for a commitment proceeding are deductible medical expenses (*Gerstacher v. Comm'r.*, 414 F.2d 448 (6th Cir. 1969)).
* Outlays for elevators, pools, etc. and other capital improvements required for medical reasons may be deductible but only to the extent that they do not add value to the property. Reg. 1.213-1(e).
* In the case of divorced parents, a child is considered the dependent of both; IRC § 213(d)(5).
* Medical expenses are not deductible if paid by insurance. IRC § 213(a).
* Child care expenses incurred while a parent is sick are not deductible.

Taylor v. Comm'r., 54 T.C.M. 129 (1987).
Taxpayer attempted to deduct the cost of having his lawn mowed, because allergies prevented him from doing so himself (this was doctor recommended).
Held: Cost of mowing the lawn was not an "expense of medical care." Fees are not deducible.

Ochs v. Comm'r., 195 F.2d 692 (2d Cir. 1952)
A mother became sick and sent her children away to school, rather than going to a sanitarium herself.
Held: That this was not deductible as a medical expense. Rather, this was a non-deductible family expense under IRC § 262 instead of an expense directly related to the patient.
Dissent argued that the cost of school should be deductible since the same result is achieved as sending mother away.

b. Clothing Expense

* If under an objective standard, work clothing may be reasonably worn outside the job, a deduction is denied even if the taxpayer subjectively would not wear them outside of work.

* Special clothes, safety gloves, helmet are deductible if they can not be worn for non-business purposes.
Military uniforms are only deductible if worn as a member of the armed forces reserve (not active duty). Reg § 1.162-2(c)(5).

Pevsner v. Comm'r, 628 F. 2d 467 (5th Cir. 1980)
A taxpayer was employed by YSL clothing boutique and was expected to wear YSL clothes at work. TP deducted cost of clothing claiming that she would not have purchased the YSL clothes if not working on her job.
Held: Denied the deduction after applying three part test:
   i.   Is clothing required as a condition of employment;
   ii. Is clothing adaptable to general usage; and
   iii. Is it so worn. In this case, it was not.

Note: If clothing is allowable, the deduction is then subject to 2% floor (IRC § 67).

c.   Legal Fees

Deduction depends on the origin and nature of the alleged liability. Personal litigation is not deductible. But, business litigation is deductible.

U.S. v. Gilmore, 372 U.S. 39 (1963)
TP attempted to deduct legal expenses from divorce suit claiming he was attempting to maintain income producing property.
Held: That this was not a deductible expense: "origin and nature" of divorce is personal.

d.   Education

   i.   Qualified scholarships: IRC § 117.

      A) GI does not include education expenses. In general when the taxpayer pays his or her own tuition, it is generally considered a personal expense. Therefore, it is not deductible.
      If one is a degree candidate at an educational organization on a qualified scholarship:
      * Qualified Scholarships only include tuition and related expenses (books, fees, supplies), not room and board.

* The exclusion from GI does *not apply to* any funds received in exchange for work by student or that is dependent upon, or is a condition for receipt of the money.

B) GI does not include any qualified tuition reduction, provided:
* It is given to an "employee" of an organization below graduate level
* Employee as defined in IRC § 132, includes, retired and disabled former employees, widows and spouse and dependent children
* Teaching or research assistants can get an exclusion even if in graduate school.

IRC § 127 provides that an employee, a spouse or dependents of an employee, may exclude up to $5,250 of benefits under a written non-discriminatory educational assistance plan, which is in effect during the taxable year. Substantial limitations are imposed on benefits for employee-owners of closely held business entities.

Note: Apart from "constructive dividend" argument, employer's contributions to an educational assistance plan should be fully deductible as ordinary and necessary business expenses under IRC § 162.

IRC § 127 expired on June 30, 1997.

However, under the "1997 Act" IRC § 127 *was extended* to permit the provision of educational benefits to taxpayer's through May 31, 2000.

ii. Non-deductible Educational Costs.
Reg § 1.162-5(b)(2)(3) In general, costs that either qualify the taxpayer for a new trade or business or that constitute the minimum educational requirement to qualify for a job are **not** deductible.

However, expenses paid or incurred by a taxpayer *may* be deductible, provided they do not violate either of the preceding conditions. That is, they neither qualify taxpayer for new trade or business nor constitute minimum educational requirements. And the education falls within the following rules:

- A) maintains or improves skills required in job (continuing education)
- B) meets express requirements of taxpayer's employer as a condition for retention of the job status or rate of compensation.

Contra: A lawyer engaged in practice can deduct continuing education expenses to improve or polish her existing skills. On the other hand, a law student cannot deduct law school classes because the education is needed to meet minimum requirement for employment.

Carroll v. Comm'r, 418 F. 2d 91 (7th Cir. 1969)
No deductions allowed for education expenses which are not related to or required by the taxpayer's job.
Held: Police officer could not deduct the expense of his pre-law classes because they were not sufficiently tied to his job.

e. Entertainment

IRC § 274 exists solely to limit or completely disallow otherwise deductible business expenses. In fact the cost of "Travel and Entertainment (T & E)" is deducible only where the taxpayer can establish that the expenses were **directly related** to the act or conduct of a trade or business or **associated with the conduct of that business.** In any event, only 50% of a substantiated meal or entertainment expense may be deducted. (IRC § 274 (n)). For purposes of IRC § 274(a), an activity entered into by the taxpayer for profit is treated on par with a trade or business activity.

   i.   Disallowance of Certain Entertainment and Other Expenses: IRC § 274.

Note:
If a person travels for sufficient business purpose as long as the dominant purpose for the trip is business, there is nothing wrong with "enjoying business travel and/or getting personal pleasure from it." However, problems occur when there are

significant personal interests in addition to business purpose for the travel.

* The cost of getting there and back, food and lodging is deductible. There is nothing wrong with enjoying this travel. However, problems occur when there are significant personal interests in the business travel.
* There is always a fine line between IRC § 162 "ordinary and necessary" test and IRC § 274 directly related test
* To be deductible, an entertainment expense must meet the requirements of **both** IRC § 162 and IRC § 274.
  1) the expense must be an ordinary and necessary business expense under IRC § 162, and
  2) the expense must be either **directly related** to or **associated with** the **active conduct** of the taxpayer's business.

A) No Deduction Unless Directly Related to Business.

IRC § 274 (a) Generally, no deduction for any entertainment amusement or recreation activity is allowed unless it is directly related to a bona fide business meeting or associated with the active conduct of taxpayer's trade or business.

* No deduction for a recreational facility --yacht, hunting lodge or for dues paid for any clubs.
* Trade = IRC § 212 activity for profit.

B) Gifts to Employees.

IRC § 274(b) Gifts to employees that are excluded under IRC § 102; employer is limited to $25 deduction.

Note: Where the employee can demonstrate another basis for the exclusion, e.g., as a "fringe benefit" IRC § 132, the limitation of IRC 274(b) is inapplicable.

C) Foreign Travel.

IRC § 274(c) Foreign Travel-- no deduction for the portion not allocable to TP's business or trade unless travel does not exceed one week or amounts to less then 25% of time not allocable to business.

* *See* IRC § 162 traveling expenses pursuant to while away from home are deductible.

D) Accurate Record-Keeping.

IRC § 274(d) The taxpayer must accurately substantiate all deductions with accurate record keeping. This is especially true of travel and entertainment ("T&E") deductions". IRC § 274(d). Reg. § 1.274-5T(a); *Cohan v. Comm'r*, 39 F.2d 401 Cir. 1930).

E) Exceptions to Business Related Expenses.

IRC § 274(e) Specific Exceptions *to Directly Related and Associated with trade or business Requirements* IRC §§ 274(e)(1)-(9)):
* Food and beverages to employee furnished on premises
* Recreation for all employees
* Employee or stockholder meetings
* Expenses related to attending business leagues, meetings and conventions under IRC § 501
* Entertainment sold to customers
* Expenses for goods, services etc. made available to the public
* Expenses, such as prizes or awards that are included in the GI of persons other than employees

F) Foreign Conventions

IRC § 274(h) Foreign conventions (IRC § 274(h))--No deduction for conventions outside of North America unless:
* meeting is directly related to active conduct of trade, business or investment
* it is as reasonable for the meeting to take place outside of North America as it is to take place within.

Look To:
* The purpose of the meeting; activities taking place there; residences of the active members; places where other meetings have been held
* The deductions for meetings on cruise ships unless sailing between American Ports.

G) Employee Achievement Awards

IRC § 274(j) Employee Achievement Awards---Cost of awards to employees for length of service or safety achievement awards up to $400 are deductible.

Note: With a qualified plan established in writing, TP can deduct up to $1600 for amounts paid to any one employee.

Note also: If the cost of plan award is deductible by the employer, the employee may exclude the value of the award under IRC § 74(c).

H) Business Meals

IRC § 274(k) Business Meals--cannot be deducted at all, unless:
    1)   the meals are not extravagant and
    2)   an employee or the taxpayer, is present

Maximum of 50% of meal and entertainment expense is allowed under any circumstances (IRC § 274(n)).

I) Entertainment Tickets.

IRC § 274(l) Entertainment Tickets--deduction cannot exceed the face value of the ticket
* If luxury box seats bought for more than one event, can only deduct up to the face value of non-luxury seats.

J) Travel.

IRC § 274(m):
* No deduction allowed for travel as a form of education (e.g., French teacher visiting France). IRC § 274(m)(2).
* Transportation is entirely deductible as long as it is primarily business.
* No deduction for a spouse or dependent traveling unless they are an employee on bona fide business purpose. Otherwise no deduction is allowed. IRC § 274(m)(3)

* Spouse assisting in entertainment is no longer a sufficient business expense. IRC § 274(m)(3).
* IRC § 274(n) Only 50% of meals and entertainment expenses are allowable as deduction (*See* IRC § 274(k), discussed *supra*).
* Except: food provided to crew members, moving expenses

Henderson v. Comm'r, 46 T.C.M. 566 (1983)
Office decorations (plant & picture) were not ordinary and necessary business expenses in the public sector since she was not trying to attract clients.
Held: Denied $100 deduction
* Must find sufficient nexus between expenses and the carrying on of business for § 162 deductions to apply.

Rudolph v U.S., 370 U.S. 269 (1962)
Taxpayer received trip as a bonus.
Held: Must include in GI;
However if the primary purpose was business then it could be deductible as a business expense.

Note:
Look at the dominant motive of the taxpayer, short business meeting with lots of pleasure (free time) is not deductible.

Schultz v. Comm'r., 16 T.C. 401 (1951)
Entertaining clients was an ordinary & necessary expense in the jewelry business.
Held: That this deduction is allowed was an approximation of the expenses.
Today: Court requires substantiation of entertainment expenses. *See* Reg § 1.274-5y(a).

Levine v. Comm'r, 51 T.C.M. 651   1986
Failure to keep an accounting of entertainment expenses in compliance with IRC § 274(d) results in loss of any deduction.
* Estimates are insufficient.

Moss v. Comm'r, 758 F.2d 211 (7th Cir. 1985)
Firm had daily lunch at an expensive restaurant in order to discuss business.
Held: That meals were not deductible. Meals were not an integral part of the conduct of the business. Court was

probably influenced by the inherently personal nature of the activity (i.e., eating and the fact that the meeting took place in a restaurant virtually on every business day of the year).

Note:
* IRC § 119 might have applied to exclude the value of the meals, but the taxpayer did not satisfy a business purpose for the meetings.

Danville Plywood Corp. v. Comm'r, 16 CL. CT 584 (1989).
Sent employees, customers, spouses and children to the super-bowl.
Held: Trip expenses related to the super-bowl trip did not satisfy either requirement under IRC § 274.

NOTE: *For an entertainment expense to be deductible, it must be both "ordinary and necessary" under § 162 and "directly related to" or "associated with" under § 274.*

Examples and Analysis:
Example 1: A media executive (TP) takes a client to dinner. To be deductible, the meal must be an "ordinary and necessary" business expense (IRC § 162). If TP passes the (IRC §162) hurdle, TP then reaches the IRC § 274(a) threshold. TP then asks: Was the expense "directly related" or "associated with" the conduct of the executive's trade or business? Finally, IRC § 274(n)(1)(A) places a limit of 50% of the meal expense allowed to be deducted, provided the expense is not extravagant.

Example 2: TP is a sole proprietor of a business and takes several clients to dinner, with a total bill of $200. TP can deduct $100 (after passing ordinary and necessary test, *supra*). There is no concern with the 2% floor because this is a non-employee expense. Therefore, it is taken above-the-line.

f.   Meals:

   i.   Meals with associates and wherein one pays for one's self, generally, are not deductible. (*But see* IRC § 119 and IRC §132 *de minimis* fringe).

ii. Employers who pay for employees pass the IRC § 162 hurdle, then reach the IRC § 274(n) threshold. For employees, a free meal is income under IRC § 61. But IRC § 119 meals on premises and IRC §132 *de minimis* fringe/working condition is to benefit the employer.

iii. Eating with a customer or client (under IRC § 162 and IRC § 274) is included in GI of the employee unless the primary purpose is to benefit the firm.

g. Traveling Expenses: **IRC § 162.**
IRC § 162(a)(2) States that reasonable traveling expenses incurred while **away from home** in pursuit of a trade or business are deductible.

Note:
If TP travels (commute) every day to get to work, cost of commutation is not deductible because it is TP's personal choice to live away from work.

Flowers v. Comm'r, 326 U.S. 465 (1945)
TP lived in Jackson and worked in Mobile, 250 miles away.

Held: It was taxpayer's personal choice to live far from work. Thus, the cost of commuting was not deductible.
Developed a three part test:
i. reasonable and necessary
ii. while away from home
iii. in pursuit of business/trade

Hantzis v. Comm'r., 638 F.2d 248 (1stCir.1981)
A law student found a job in New York for the summer but lived with her husband in Boston. She lived in a temporary home in NY and maintained their Boston home.
Held: That there was no business purpose to keep permanent home. Therefore the cost of temporary housing although away from "home" in "pursuit of business" was not deductible.

* One would need a business connection to both cities in order to justify having 2 homes and deducting one or both.
* If an employer temporarily assigns employee (TP) to another area, then TP can deduct food, transportation and lodging.

There is no need for TP to uproot her family to get the deduction providing TP has business ties to both places.
* For purposes of IRC § 162, work in another place for over a year no longer equals a *temporary home.* Then, employment at the new location is indefinite and travel costs become non deductible.

Note:
IRC § 217 provides a deduction for moving expenses if job adds at least 35 miles to commute.

Note also: If an employee's moving expenses are reimbursed by an employer, it is possible for the employee to exclude the amount of the reimbursement, provided the expenses would have been deductible under IRC §217.

h. Personal, Living and Family Expenses: **IRC § 262.**

   i.   In General
   IRC § 262(a) Except as otherwise provided, there is no deduction for personal, living or family expenses.

   ii. Telephone Service
   IRC § 262(b) Any charge for basic telephone service for the first telephone line in any residence is a personal expense.

   Notwithstanding the fact that they are inherently personal, some expenses are deductible, such as mortgage interest (IRC § 163), real property taxes (IRC § 164), casualty losses (IRC § 165(c)(3), (h)), bad debts (IRC § 166) and investment losses (IRC § 165(f), 1211(b)). However, in order to be deductible, most personal/yet deductible items are required to be expended in connection with a trade or business of the taxpayer (IRC § 162) or an income-producing activity of the taxpayer (IRC § 212). These requirements have led some of the more creative taxpayers to attempt to convert a recreational activity or "hobby," such as having a pet, into a "business-like" activity, such as dog-breeding. One of the sections that patrols "for abuse in this area" is IRC § 183.

   iii. Activities not engaged in for profit: IRC § 183
   IRC § 183(a) Disallow all deductions for an individual or S corporation for activities not engaged in for profit.

iv. Deductions Allowed: IRC § 183(b)
Deductions are allowed for:
  A) "Otherwise allowable" deductions (mortgage interest, real property, taxes, etc.)
  B) A deduction is allowed as though activity were engaged in for profit, but only to the extent that the gross income derived from such activity for the taxable year exceeds the deductions allowed in subparagraph 1) above.

v. *Bottom line:*
"*Not otherwise allowable*"" deductions, such as depreciation, are allowable only to the extent of any Gross Income derived from a "Not-for-Profit" activity, reduced by allocable mortgage interest and taxes.

vi. Income and Loss from Hobbies:
Expenses for "hobbies," i.e., activities which are neither related to a taxpayer's trade or business or an income producing activity, are non-deductible.

Example:

Dr. Armstrong, a pediatrician, runs a dog-breeding facility as a hobby. In the current taxable year she pays $X .00 for feed, entry fees for competitions and veterinarians expenses. During the year, her dogs won prizes totaling an aggregate of $X.00. She also paid real property taxes of $X.00 and mortgage interest of $X.00.
Dr. Armstrong can deduct the real property taxes and mortgage interest in full. However, assuming her dog-breeding activity does not rise to the level of a trade or business or income producing activity, her expenses for depreciation, feed, and veterinarians fees are deductible only to the extent of the gross income from such activities (the prize money of $X.00, *as reduced by* the otherwise allowable expenses of $X.00 (the mortgage interest and real property taxes).

NOTE: IRC § 103(d) *Presumption*:: The activity is *for profit* if it has been profitable for the past three of five years or (two of seven years if major part of the activity is for breeding, training, etc. of horses).

91

Note also: Hobby loss is limited to hobby income.

Nickerson v. Comm'r, 700 F2d 402 (7th Cir. 1983)
Taxpayer purchased a farm with the hope of generating additional income. **TP did not expect a profit for several years. Comm'r. disallowed TP's deduction of expenses claiming the TP's primary goal in operating the farm was not to make a profit.**
Held: Facts demonstrated sufficient profit motive for characterization. To be "profit minded," profit does not have to be immediate, long-run profitability, even though a loss is sufficient.

Note:
Relevant factors of a "For Profit" activity, (Reg. § 1.183-2(b))
No set formula:
* Manner taxpayer carries out the activity
* Expertise of taxpayer and advisors
* Time and effort expended
* Expectation that assets will appreciate in value
* Success in carrying out similar / dissimilar activities
* History of income or loss with regard to the activity
* Elements of pleasure, recreation
* Amount of profits earned
* Financial status of taxpayer

3. Interest

    a. Basic Requirements
        In general, interest on taxpayer's debt may be deducted, subject to limitations. Interest on investment or business debt is deductible with limits for Trade, Business, Investment and Mortgage, subject to the following conditions:
        i.   must be the debt of TP, even without personal liability (i.e., debt may be recourse with taxpayer's personal liability or nonrecourse without personal obligation); and
        ii. must be bona fide debt and not:
             A) sham
             B) Without economic substance - no possibility of gain or loss
             C) property worth less than the debt with nonrecourse loan, the debtor cannot take an interest deduction on any part of the loan (*Estate of Franklin v. Comm'r.,*

544 F.2d 1045 (9th Cir. 1976)); or TP allowed to deduct interest to the extent of the property value (*Pleasant Summit Land Corp. v. Comm'r.*, 863 F.2d 263 (3d Cir. 1988))
  D) business purpose

Note: Family loans are highly scrutinized

b. Limits on Deduction.

IRC § 163 Interest

IRC § 163(a) Allows a deduction for all interest paid or accrued in the taxable year on indebtedness, subject to specific limitations.

IRC § 163(d)(1) Investment Interest -- Limits deduction for "investment interest," i.e., any interest allowable as a deduction which is paid or accrued on investment debt (IRC § 163(h)(3)(A)).

For the taxable year:
Net investment income = Investment income *minus* Investment expenses

Carry-forward - If it is "excess" investment interest, then it is not taken as a deduction for this year. It can be carried over to next year. (IRC § 163(d)(2)).

IRC § 163(h)(1) Interest on personal debt is not deductible, with the exception of a deduction for qualified residence interest.

IRC § 163(h)(2) Personal Interest--Deductions only for:

IRC § 163(h)(3) Qualified Residence *Interest*:
* Acquisition -- (Deductible)
* Indebtedness from building, buying, improving, or refinancing a qualified residence that is secured by such residence
* Limited to $1,000,000 ($500,000 if married, filing separate returns)
* Home Equity Indebtedness--(Deductible)
  Any other debt secured by the qualified residence (2d mortgage) can't exceed total of $100,000 or $50,000 in the case of a separate return by a married individual.
  Or the FMV-*reduced by* acquisition debt.

IRC § 163 (h)(4)(a) Principal or second residence used by the taxpayer or a family member as a residence
* Dollar limitations determined per taxpayer, not per household.
* Married individuals are treated as one taxpayer

Note:
* Interest is allocated by the *use* of the proceeds.
* Because some interest is not deductible, borrowed money must be traced to actual use. Commingled funds sometimes makes this difficult.

Example and Analysis:
Taxpayer (TP) purchased a residence for $1,500,000. TP made a $50,000 down payment and took a mortgage loan for $1,450,000. The deduction for interest on acquisition debt is limited to $1,000,000 (for a married couple filing a joint return) of such debt IRC § 163(h)(3). Thus, the interest allocable to the *balance* of $400,000 on the mortgage debt is not deductible.

Note:
Suppose the house subsequently appreciates in value to $1.6 million and the TP-homeowner subsequently borrows an additional $150,000 using the equity in the house as collateral. Then, in that case, the additional home equity loan is deductible, only up to $100,000 IRC § 163(h)(3)(C).

4. Taxes
State & Local, Foreign, Personal Property, and Real Estate taxes can be deducted.

IRC § 164 Taxes

IRC § 164(a) The following taxes are allowed as a deduction:

IRC § 164(b) State, local & foreign "real property " income taxes, war profits and excess profits taxes; state & local personal property taxes; GST (Generation-skipping transfer tax) on income distributions; IRC § 59A environmental taxes;
* Any State, local or foreign taxes paid or accrued in carrying out a trade or business or IRC § 212 activity (excise, import social security on employers, gas, etc.)

* Any tax paid or accrued on the acquisition or disposition of property is treated as part of the cost or reduction of the amount realized from a sale.

IRC § 164(c) The following taxes are entirely nondeductible Federal income, social security, federal estate & gift taxes, state inheritance tax.
* No deduction for taxes on special assessment.
* No deduction for sales tax and personal taxes
* User fees for park services, etc. are nondeductible

5. Personal Deductions: Charitable and Other Contributions and Gifts : **IRC § 170.**

Deduction is allowed for a charitable contribution when contributed with detached and disinterested generosity. The contribution must be to non-profit and non-political organizations.

Where the taxpayer transfers property to a trust in which the benefits are split between one or more charitable entities and "private" (i.e., non charitable interests), special restrictions apply. Failure to comply with these restrictions even in a relatively minor technical way may mean complete loss of the charitable contribution. The "1997 Act" tightens these restrictions.
In the case of an individual, deductions for contributions to the following organizations are limited to 50% of the taxpayer's contribution base, but there is a limited (5-year) carry-forward of "excess". IRC § 170(k).

Contribution Base = AGI before net operating loss (IRC § 172).

Contributions to entities that Qualify as Charities (IRC § 170(b)):
The following organizations may be the recipient of deductible charitable donations subject to a limitation of 50% of the taxpayer's contribution base.
* Church
* Educational organization with regular curriculum students and faculty
* Organization where the principal purpose is providing medical or hospital care or medical education or research, as long as the organization is committed to spending the money by January 1 five years later

* Organization that receives a substantial amount of support from the U.S. or one of the state subdivisions or public contributions and is organized for the benefit of a college or University
* A "Governmental Unit" organized under a governmental, state or a political subdivision for public purposes
* A private Foundation under a Corporation, Community Chest, Fund or Foundation created in the US or under US laws, organized and operated exclusively for religious, charitable, scientific, literary, or educational purposes or to foster amateur sports (providing facilities or equipment) or prevention of cruelty to children and animals
* Organization of War Veterans founded under US laws
* Gift by an individual to a fraternity, lodge, order or association if used exclusively for religious, charitable, scientific, literary, educational purposes or prevention of cruelty to children and animals
* Cemetery companies

Contributions to other charitable entities (the "B" charities) are also deductible. However, this is only to the extent that such contributions do not exceed the lesser of 30% of the contribution base for the year or 50% of the **excess of such contribution** over contributions to the "A" charities, identified above (i.e., the charities to which contributions may be made). In addition, deductions calculated are subject to a limit of 50% of TP's contribution base.

Substantiation requirement (IRC § 170(f)(8)):
* Contribution must be made to a qualified charitable organization
* Any contribution over $250 in cash, or a contribution of goods valued at $75 or more or services received must be substantiated by a contemporaneous written acknowledgment by the donee
* List amount of cash and description of the property and whether the organization supplied any goods or services in exchange, and their value
* Gift of property = FMV at the time of the gift
* Not required for publicly traded stock
* Appraisal must be done by a qualified expert

Notes:
* General Rule-Deduction for charitable contribution of property is the FMV or property at time of the contribution.
* IRC § 170 encourages charity --No tax is paid on gain for donated property (better to donate than to sell as a (bargained sale) - deduct the FMV and do not recognize the gain). However, this rule is subject to very substantial limitations with regard to contributions

of "ordinary income" or "short-term assets" (IRC § 170(e)(1)(A)) and property contributed to a charity for a use inconsistent with the basis upon which the charity is exempt from a tax (IRC § 170(e)(1)(B)).

* To be deductible, payment must be made in the taxable year, not merely pledged
* The organization's own immunity from taxation is determined by IRC § 501(c)
* Organizations engaged in lobbying will lose their tax exempt status. This is not a first amendment violation since First Amendment does not guarantee subsidy for free speech *(Regan v. Taxation / representation of Washington,* 461 U.S. 540 (1983)
* Personal services (celebrity appearance, blood) are not deductible
* *Voluntariness* : Making a contribution in lieu of a jail term is not deductible (*Lombardo v. Comm'r.,* WL15175 CT. C. (1985).
* If a taxpayer makes a donation to a University which entitles him to purchase season tickets for sporting events not otherwise available, then only 80% of contribution is deductible
* Contributions made for participation in religious services are deductible (e.g., seats, pews, etc.) (*Powell v. U.S.,* 945 F.2d 374 (11th Cir. 1991).
* In *Bargain Sales* of property to a charity at a decreased price, the difference between selling price and FMV is deductible
* No deduction to the extent that a benefit is received but detached and disinterested generosity is required.
* Question to Ask: Did the donor receive a substantial benefit from the transfer. Therefore is the transfer more a like a *quid pro quo* transaction than a gift?

Ottawa Sillica v. U.S., 699 F.2d 1124 (Fed. Cir. 1983)
Corporation donated a large parcel of land to build a school expecting that the school would build a road which would make the rest of its property more valuable.
Held: Not deductible as a donation since the taxpayer received a benefit

* A taxpayer who anticipates receipt of substantial benefits in return for a charitable contribution cannot claim a deduction under IRC § 170.

* Services Performed for Charities:
  ⇒ A taxpayer can work for charity for free without being taxed on the value of the serviced rendered. However, income from employment cannot be diverted into charity.
  ⇒ Thus, if TP diverts compensation payment to charity, TP is still taxed on it, because TP is deemed to have *constructively* received it and *then* contributed it. Deduction is limited to the TP's contribution base percentage IRC § 170(k).

Schuster v. Comm'r, 800 F.2d 672 (7th Cir. 1986)
A nurse, who was a nun, was taxed on her salary even though she donated it all pursuant to her vow of poverty.

6. Tax consequences of divorce

   a. Alimony and Separate Maintenance Payments: In General

   IRC § 61(a)(8) Alimony and separate maintenance payments are each included in GI of the payee.

   > **Notice** of new tax developments as of July 10, 1998: One of the proposed changes effective upon the President signing into law effects the former spouse: Divorced taxpayers will be able to avoid paying for tax mistakes caused without their knowledge by former spouses.

   * Alimony is a post marital continuation of support required of a spouse during marriage

   * Child support is not included in the GI of payee (nor deductible to payor) since there is a continued obligation to support one's children. In effect, child support is a personal expense (within IRC § 262), of the payor spouse and therefore is not deductible.

   If one receives Alimony = Pay Taxes

   If one receives child support = Tax Free

   If one pays Alimony = Deduction

   If one pays child support = No Deduction

b.   Alimony: Allowable Deductions

IRC § 215   Alimony and Other Payments

IRC § 215(a) Deduction is allowed for an amount equal to the alimony or separate maintenance paid during the taxable year pursuant to a "divorce or separation instrument."

IRC § 215(c)(1) Identification number requirement: Any individual who receives spousal support is required to furnish his/her social security number to the payor. The payor must include it on his/her return. Failure to do so triggers a $50 penalty.

Note:
*   Child support is not deductible because of the continued obligation to support one's children, an inherently personal non-deductible expense. See IRC § 215(g)(1)(D) (specifically denying any deductions for child support payments). *Compare* IRC § 262 (denying a deduction for "personal, living and family expenses"). *See* discussion, *infra.*

c.   Alimony: Scope of Limitations

IRC § 71 Alimony and separate maintenance payments

IRC § 71(a) GI includes amounts paid as alimony or separate maintenance payments. To constitute alimony, a payment must be:
  i.   In cash (§71(b)(1));
  ii.   Received by or on behalf of a spouse under a divorce or separation instrument (§71(b)(1)(A));
  iii. The instrument does not designate the payment as **not includible in the recipient's gross income and not deductible under §215** (§71(b)(1)(C));
  iv.   Where the parties are legally separated under a decree of divorce or of separate maintenance, the spouses must **not** be members of the same household at the time the payment is made. §71(b)(1)(C).;
  v.   **NOTE** This limitation does not apply to couples who are merely separated pursuant to a written Separation Agreement (Reg. § 1.71-1T, Q and A9);
  vi.   There can be no liability to pay alimony after the death of the payee spouse, or any liability to make any payment as

a substitute for such payments after the death of such payee spouse. §71(b)(1)(D); and

vii. The parties do not file a joint tax return.

CAUTION: Informal separations do not shift tax consequences. To accomplish such a shift, the payments must be pursuant to a "divorce or separation instrument which includes any of the following:

A) a decree of divorce or separation maintenance or a written instrument incident to such a decree (§71(b)(2)(A));

B) a written separation agreement (§71(b)(2)(B)); or

C) a decree not described in §71(b)(2)(A) which requires a spouse to make payments for the support or maintenance of the other spouse.

IRC § 215 provides that alimony or separate maintenance payments paid during the taxable year are deductible "above-the-line" by the payor spouse.

d.   Alimony v. Child Support Payments.

IRC § 152(e) - Child Support. Payments to support children of the marriage do not constitute alimony. Child support is excluded from the GI of the payee spouse and the payor spouse gets no deduction. Custodial parent controls exemption.

IRC § 71(c)(1). Child support is that amount which the divorce or separation instrument **fixes** in terms of an amount of money or as part of payment as a sum which is payable for the support of the children of the payor spouse.

IRC § 71(c)(2) states that if an instrument provides for a reduction in the amount of any payment:

i.   on the *happening of a contingency specified in the instrument relating to a child* (such as attaining a specified age, marrying, dying, leaving school or a similar contingency); or

ii. at a time which *can clearly be associated* with a contingency of a kind specified (in the preceding sub-paragraph); or

    iii. An amount equal to such reduction will be treated
as *an amount fixed as payable* for the support of
the children of the payor spouse.

Reminder:
IRC § 71(c)(1). The distinction between child support and
alimony is critical because child support is excluded from GI of
payor spouse and custodial parent controls dependency exemption.

IRC § 71(c)(2). If any amount of money due under the
instrument is reduced due to *a contingency relating to a child* (i.e.,
child's age, marriage or death, etc.) the amount paid will be treated
as child support.

"If any amount of money due under a divorce or separation
instrument" is reduced due to a contingency relating to a child (age,
marriage, death, etc.), the amount paid will be treated as non-
taxable, non-deductible child support. IRC § 71(c)(2)(A).

IRC § 71(c)(3). If the payor spouse fails to satisfy all
obligations for alimony and child support, any future payments
must be allocated to child support first. Thus, there is no incentive
in the statute to delay payment of alimony and child support
payments because they are first allocable to a non-deductible item,
child support.

    e. "Recapture" of Excess Front-Loaded Alimony.

IRC § 71(f). "Recapture" of excess front loaded alimony
payments

IRC § 71(f) requires that "excess front-loaded alimony" be
"recaptured" in the third post-separation year (i.e., in the third year
in which the spouses are separated/divorced) pursuant to the
provisions of IRC §§ 71 and 215.

Excess front-loaded alimony comprises the sum of excess payments
for:
    i. The first post-separation year; and
    ii. The second post-separation year.

IRC § 71(f)(6). Essentially, the statute penalizes excessive alimony payments in the early years of a schedule of payments. In fact, the statute focuses on a very compressed time period: the first three years following the couple's divorce or separation to which §§ 71 and 215 apply. IRC § 71(f)(6).

"Recapture" is a concept used throughout the Internal Revenue Code, but it means different things in different contexts. It may mean something quite different to the Payor spouse than to the Payee spouse. Alimony recapture does not involve, as IRC §§ 1245 and 1250 do, *a recharacterization* of income nor does it involve *an actual repayment* of the "excess" alimony. Nonetheless, it can be a substantially disruptive element in an otherwise carefully planned alimony and property settlement agreement.

IRC § 71(f)(1) provides that if there are "excess payments" of alimony in the first and/or second post-separation years, the amount of such excess is to be "recaptured" in the third post-separation year.

When alimony is "recaptured," the excess alimony is included in the payor spouse's GI for the third post-separation year and the payee spouse gets an "above-the-line" deduction in that year.

This has the potential for substantial adverse tax consequences to both the payor spouse and payee spouse of the excess alimony. For the payor spouse, excess alimony paid must be included in his/her gross income for the third post-separation year. For the payee spouse, the recaptured alimony is deductible presumably "above-the-line." However, if the payee does not have sufficient income, then he/she cannot take full advantage of the deduction granted by the statute. *See* example, *infra.*

"Front-Loading" involves paying *more* alimony in earlier years and less later on. IRS's concern is that taxpayers will disguise a nondeductible payment, such as spouse's legal fees or a property settlement as alimony.

Computing "Recapture."
Recapture of the amount of ordinary income to the payor and a deduction to the payee is computed through a series of mind-numbing steps, as follows.

IRC §§ 71(f)(3) and 71(f)(4). **"Recapture"** means that the "excess front-loaded alimony" for the first and second post-separation years will be "recaptured" in the third post-separation year. The *amount recaptured* is the sum of excess alimony for the first post-separation year and the second post-separation year. When the alimony paid in the first "post-separation year" exceeds the average of payments in the second and third post-separation years, by more than $15,000, the excess is labeled as "excess alimony" for the first post-separation year. Though, "recapture" is postponed until the third post-separation year.

IRC § 71(f)(4) "Recapture" for the second post-separation year. Similarly, if payments in the second post-separation year exceed those in the third post-separation year by more than $15,000, the excess is "recaptured" in the third year.

Note: The amount of "excess" alimony that is recaptured in the third post-separation year consists of excess alimony for the first post-separation year and the second post-separation year. The nature of the calculation demands that excess alimony for the second year be computed first. IRC §§71(f)(1) and (2).

Excess Alimony for Second Post-Separation Year. Excess alimony for the Second Post-Separation Year consists of simply comparing the amount paid, as alimony, in Years 2 and 3 of the Post-Separation period. To the extent that such amounts in Year 2 exceed those in Year 3, plus *$15,000* (can be viewed as sort of a statutory de minimis zone), there is an *excess amount to be recaptured.*
NOTE: If there is no such excess, or amounts paid in Year 3 exceed those paid in Year 2, there simply is no recapture for Year 2.

Excess Alimony for First Year. This calculation is considerably more complex than the Year 2 computation in part because it takes the results of the Year 2 calculation into account in determining the excess alimony attributable to the First Post-Separation Year.

Example 1:
The computation of "excess alimony payments" may be illustrated in the following examples. As part of a settlement of their property rights, husband (H) and wife (W), who have no children, agree that H will pay alimony to W as follows:

Year   1   - $100,000
Year   2   - $ 70,000
Year   3   - $ 30,000
Year   4 and thereafter - no obligation to make alimony payments.

On these facts, there is "excess alimony" of $72,500, computed as follows:

Excess alimony for second post-separation year:
Alimony paid in the second post-separation year ($70,000) minus alimony paid in the third post-separation year ($30,000) plus $15,000 = $45,000 resulting in $25,000 "excess" alimony for the second post-separation year.

Excess alimony for the first post-separation year:
$47,500 (alimony paid in first post-separation year ($100,000) *minus* average of alimony paid in second post-separation year ($70,000) less $25,000 of already "recaptured" alimony = $45,000 of alimony attributable to second post-separation year plus alimony attributable to third post-separation year ($30,000) = $75,000 average for second and third years = $37,500 average plus $15,000 = $52,500; alimony paid in first post-separation year exceeds this sum by $47,500. Total alimony recaptured is $47,500. ($47,500 Year One + $25,000 Year Two = $72,500).

In year 1 - H pays $100,000 as alimony. W includes this amount in her gross income. H deducts the alimony above-the-line (IRC §§ 215, 62(a)(15).

In year 2 - The alimony paid by H ($70,000) is includible in W's gross income and deductible by H. There is no concern recapture at this point. Recapture occurs only in the third post-separation year.

H deducts the alimony paid in the second post-separation year ($70,000) and W include the amount. Recapturing alimony, if any, is not calculated until Year 3.

In year 3 - H pays and W includes $30,000. H takes above-the-line deduction for this amount and W includes this in GI.

In addition, H includes $72,500 of "Recaptured" alimony and W deducts this amount. A detailed illustration of the calculation of "excess alimony follows:

Alimony for the Second Post-Separation Year:

The Excess of

1) $70,000   Alimony paid in the second post-separation year

over
2) $45,000   Alimony paid in the third post-separation year
                     + $15,000 ($30,000 + $15,000 = $45,000)

3) $25,000   Excess Alimony for second post-separation year

Alimony for the First Post-Separation Year:

1) $100,000   Alimony paid in the first post-separation year
over the average of

2) $ 45,000   Alimony paid in the second post-separation year
                     ($70,000) less previously recaptured ($25,000)
                     ($70,000 - $25,000 = $45,000)

3) $ 30,000   Alimony for second post-separation year

    $37,500

4)+ $15,000

    $52,500

5) $47,500   Alimony for first post-separation year

    $72,500   Total excess front-loaded alimony
                     (Steps 3 & 5)

Example 2: The facts are the same as in the previous example, except that the alimony payments to be paid are in reverse order. The husband is obligated to pay $30,000 in year 1, $70,000 in year 2, and $100,000 in year 3. **Here, there is no "recapture" of alimony although the aggregate amount of alimony paid or to be paid ($200,000) during the year to former spouse remains precisely the same.** The reason for this result is that alimony does not fall off; rather it increases. This is permissible under the statute. Similarly, if the alimony to be paid in the first three post-separation years was $200,000 and was divided evenly among the first 3 years, there again would be no recapture for the same reason: the absence of a fall off in alimony paid.

Note:
Recapture rules do not apply if:
  i.   payment of alimony cease due to death or remarriage of either spouse prior to the end of the third post-separation year. IRC § 71(f)(5)(A),
  ii.   the alimony is paid pursuant to a temporary support order described in IRC § 71(b)(2)(C) (IRC § 71(f)(5)(B)), or
  iii. the payments are made pursuant to a continuing liability of the payor spouse to make payments -- over a period of not less than 3 years --of a fixed portion or portions of the income from a business or property or from compensation from self-employment (IRC § 71(f)(5)(C)).

Practical Application: The "Recapture" problem can be eliminated by proper planning.

IRC § 71 does not apply if the parties file joint returns (IRC § 71(e)).

f.   Property Settlements

IRC § 1041   Transfers of property between spouses incident to divorce

IRC § 1041(a) There is no gain or loss recognized on the transfer of property between spouses or between former spouses, but in the latter case only where the transfer is "incident to divorce."

Reg. § 1.1041-1T: Transfers of property within one year of the cessation of the marriage will be treated by the IRS as subject to IRC § 1041, regardless of whether "related to the cessation of the marriage." Transfers in years 2-6 following the termination of the marriage are rebuttably presumed to be related to the cessation of the marriage, while those made more than six years later are presumed (again rebuttably) not to be "related". Reg. § 1.1041-1 T

IRC § 1041(b) Such uninterrupted transfers are treated as gifts *not* as sales or other transfers

Note:
* Transferee takes on the same basis as the transferor (no step up).
* Non-resident aliens: Not applicable if the individual making the transfer is a non resident alien

IRC § 1041(e) IRC § 1041(a) does not apply to a transfer of property in trust if the total liability assumed plus the amount of the liabilities to which the property is subject is greater than the total adjusted basis of the property transferred.

Note:
IRC § 1041 reverses result in cases, such as United States v. Davis, 370 U.S. 65 (1962)

U.S. v. Davis, 370 U.S. 65 (1962)
Gains from the transfer of property due to a marital settlement are taxable and determined by the difference between the FMV at the time of transfer.

V.   TAXABLE INCOME

A. IMPOSITION OF TAX; CALCULATION OF TAXABLE INCOME

1.   Calculating Taxable Income

IRC §1 Imposes a tax on the **Taxable Income** of married taxpayers filing joint returns, and surviving spouses (IRC § 1 (a)), heads of household (IRC § 1 (b)), unmarried taxpayers (IRC § 1 (c)), married taxpayers filing separate returns (IRC § 1 (d)) and trusts and estates (IRC § 1 (e)).

With respect to an individual taxpayer, IRC § 63 defines **Taxable Income** as **Adjusted Gross Income** *minus* either *itemized deductions* (sometimes referred to as **"Below-the-line deductions"**) or a *standard* deduction. The computation may be expressed as follows:

STEP 1:   Determine the taxpayer's **Gross Income**
STEP 2:   Subtract taxpayer's **"Above-the-Line"** deductions
             (IRC § 62; 162)
STEP 3:   Determine taxpayer's **Adjusted Gross Income**
             (Step 1 *less* Step 2)
STEP 4:   Subtract
             a)   The larger of taxpayer's:
                   (i) "Itemized" deductions (IRC § 63(d)); or
                   (ii) "Standard" deduction (IRC § 63(b));

             b)   and subtract "available personal and dependency
                   exemptions" (IRC §§ 151; 152)
STEP 5:   Compute **Taxable Income** (IRC § 63(a))
             (Step 3 less Step 4)
STEP 6:   Apply tax rates (IRC §§ 1(a)(1)-(5))
STEP 7:   Apply credits (IRC §§ 21, et. seq.) to reduce tax liability.

Calculation of Taxable Income

GI – §62 Deductions = **AGI**

AGI – Personal Exemptions and either the standard
<u>Or</u> itemized deductions = **Taxable Income**

Taxable Income x Tax Rate = **Gross Tax Liability**

Gross Tax Liability - Credits = **Net Tax Liability**

---

2.   Deductions Gets One to AGI

IRC § 62   Adjusted gross income defined

Unlike other taxpayers, an individual computes **taxable income** by subtracting from **Adjusted Gross Incomes Certain Deductions**. Thus, an individual taxpayer starts with **Gross Income** *subtracts certain* **"above-the-line"** deductions to arrive at **Adjusted Gross Income**. From this figure certain additional deductions are taken to arrive at taxable income. IRC § 62 is the exclusive source for determining "above-the-line" deductions.

3.   "Above-The-Line" Deductions

Include:

a.   Trade or business deductions, other than those paid in the taxpayer's capacity as an employee.

b.   Trade or business deductions of employees who are operating under a reimbursement or other expense allowance arrangement with the employer.

c.   Certain expenses of performing artists.

d.   Losses from sales or exchanges of property as provided in IRC §§165(f) and 1211(b)

e.   Deductions attributable to rents and royalties under IRC § 212.

f.   Certain deductions of life tenants and income beneficiaries of property.

g.   Contributions to pension, profit-sharing and annuity plans of self employed individuals.

h. Contributions to individual retirement accounts (IRAs), any deduction allowed by IRC § 402(b)(3) which represents a lump sum distribution from a pension plan.
i. Penalties forfeited because of premature withdrawal funds from time savings accounts or deposits.
j. The alimony deduction afforded by IRC § 215.
k. Certain reforestation expenses allowed by IRC § 194.
l. Certain required repayment of supplemental and unemployment compensation benefits.
m. Jury duty pay remitted to employer.
n. Deduction for clean fuel vehicles and certain refueling property allowed by IRC § 179A.
o. The moving expense deduction afforded by IRC § 217.

4. Taxable income defined: IRC § 63

IRC § 63(a) Taxable Income is defined as Adjusted Gross Income *minus either* "Itemized Deductions" or "Standard Deduction" and Personal Exemptions thus,

IRC § 63(a) Taxable income = GI - (deductions to get to AGI) - either the standard or itemized deductions) - (personal exemptions)

IRC § 63(b) If an individual chooses not to itemize his/her deductions:

Standard Deduction: the sum of the basic plus additional standard deductions:
* Joint or surviving Spouse = $6,700
* Head of Household = $5,900
* Individual = $4,400
* Married filing separately = $3,350

Taxable Income = AGI - standard deduction - personal exemptions as a deduction under IRC § 151.

Adjustments for Inflation: Since 1988, the tax rates and the amounts of the standard deduction and personal dependent exemptions have been "indexed" (i.e., adjusted to reflect increases in the consumer price index (CPI)). IRC § 1 (f).

The standard deduction for individual taxpayers is indexed in much the same manner as tax rates. See Rev. Proc. 95-53, 1995 - C.B.

5. "Below-the-line" deductions: **IRC § 63(e).**

Itemized deductions are the deductions permitted other than those allowed in determining AGI (the "above-the-line" deductions) and IRC §151 personal exemptions

Itemized Deductions may include:
* mortgage interest
* state income and property taxes
* casualty losses above 10% of AGI
* medical expenses above 7.5% of AGI
* charitable contributions
* certain business expenses of employees above 2% of AGI.

Miscellaneous itemized deductions are allowed only to the extent that the aggregate exceeds 2% of AGI (IRC § 67 (a)).

Taxpayer can take either the standard deduction or Itemized deductions

Example:
An accountant is paid $10,000 in salary and spends $100 on dues for association membership. What is his/her Taxable Income?

Analysis:
The association dues would ordinarily be deductible, if not as business expenses, then as production of income expenses (IRC § 212). However, payment of dues falls into the category of a **"miscellaneous itemized deduction"** (IRC § 67 (G)), which is not deductible until the aggregate of such deductions **exceeds two percent** of the taxpayer's AGI. Inasmuch as the association dues did not exceed two percent of AGI ($200), the dues were not deductible at all. However, if the taxpayer's Adjusted Gross Income was only $4,800, 2 percent of AGI would equal $96. Thus, $4 of the payment would qualify.

But: IRC § 67(a): In the case of an individual, miscellaneous itemized deductions are allowed only if the aggregate is greater than 2% of AGI. 2% floor *limits miscellaneous deductions* to the excess of 2% of AGI. So if dues are itemized deductions then IRC § 67(a) provides that it can't be deducted.

6. "Miscellaneous Itemized Deductions": **IRC § 67.**

Prior to 1987, as noted, deductions were classified as "above -the-line" or "below-the-line". However, starting in 1987, a new category of deductions "miscellaneous itemized deductions" was introduced in IRC § 67.
This section is devastating to most taxpayers because it subjects all but a handful of non-business deductions to an arbitrary two percent AGI "floor." This means that a deduction is allowed only to the extent that the aggregate of such items exceeds two percent of the taxpayers' AGI.

For purposes of this limitation, IRC § 67 (b) provides the following exceptions to the two percent of Adjusted Gross Income Limitation:
   a. The interest deduction under IRC § 163;
   b. The deduction for taxes under IRC § 164;
   c. Casualty losses under IRC § 165 (c)(3)(d);
   d. Charitable contributions under IRC § 170;
   e. Medical expenses under IRC §213;
   f. Any deduction allowable for impairment-related work expenses;
   g. The "section 691(c) deduction" for estate tax attributable "to income in respect of a decedent";
   h. Any deduction allowable in connection with personal property used in a short sale;
   i. The deduction under IRC § 1341 relating to the computation of tax where income is claimed as of right;
   j. The deduction allowable under IRC § 72 (b) (3) where annuity payments cease by reason of death of the annuitant;
   k. The deduction for amortizable bond premium under IRC § 171; and
   l. The deduction under IRC § 216 relating to cooperative housing corporations.

7. Overall limitations on itemized deductions: **IRC § 68** (more $ AGI = less itemized deductions).

IRC §68 (a) If a taxpayer's AGI exceeds the "applicable amount" (as defined in IRC §68 (b)), the amount of itemized deductions otherwise allowable for the taxable year shall be reduced by the *lesser* of:
   1) 3% of the excess AGI over the *applicable amount,* or
   2) 80% of the amount of the itemized deductions otherwise allowable for such taxable year.

The term *itemized deductions* does not include medical expenses, investment interest, or casualty, business, and wager loss deductions IRC § 68(c).

IRC § 68(d) provides that the limitation is to be applied "after the application of any other limitation on the allowance of any itemized deduction."

IRC § 68(e) provides that the limitation does not apply to estates and trusts.

IRC § 68(b)(1) The "applicable amount" is $100,000 ($50,000 for married taxpayers filing separately). This amount is adjusted annually for inflation, as are tax rates, standard deductions, and exemptions. *See* IRC §1(f).

Example:
A taxpayer has an adjusted gross income of $211,800. In calculating AGI, TP utilized $28,000 of itemized deductions (not including medical, investment interest, or casualty losses).
Since AGI is in excess of $100,00, the limitation of IRC § 68 is potentially applicable. The limitation is determined as follows: The itemized deductions (other than medical, investment interests or casualty losses) are reduced by the lesser of:

1) 3% of excess of AGI ($211,800) over the Applicable Amount ($100,000) = $3,354, or
2) 80% of the otherwise allowable itemized deductions $28,000 = $22,400.

Thus, the itemized deductions are reduced by $3,354. Accordingly, allowable deductions are $24,646.

IRC § 68(b)(2) Adjustments for Inflation provided by the Secretary of State.
Cost of living adjustment is the percentage which consumer price index (CPI) exceeds CPI of 1993
Rounded to the nearest multiple of $50 ($25 if married filing separately)

8.   Kiddie Tax.

Tax on minors, i.e., children, under 14 with either parent alive. Unearned income of children are taxed at the same rate as their parents "Kiddie Tax" IRC § 1(g).

For purposes of the Kiddie Tax "unearned income" is defined as income other than "wages, salaries, or professional fees and other amounts received as compensation for personal services actually rendered . . . does not include that part of the compensation derived by the taxpayer for personal services rendered . . . to a corporation which represents a distribution of earnings or profits rather than a reasonable allowance as compensation for the personal services rendered." *See* IRC § 911(d)(2).

If the child's parents are not married, the tax rate to be referenced is that of the custodial parent (IRC § 1(g)(5)(A)). If the parents are married, but filing separately, the applicable tax rate is that of the parent with the greater taxable income.
IRC § 1(g)(7) permits the parents to elect to report the income of a child on their return, subject to limitations.

Unearned income = rent, dividend, and interest not derived from personal services

*   Child uses the custodial parent rate if not married and the higher taxable income parent in the case of separate filings
*   Parents can elect to put certain unearned income of their children on their return.

9.   Maximum capital gains tax rates: (See Chapter VII: Capital Gains and Losses)

If a taxpayer has a *net capital gain*, i.e., an excess of **net long-term capital gain** over **net short-term capital loss** (IRC § 1222)(11)), which includes profits from the sale of stocks, bonds and most other investments, the tax rate on such **recognized gain** shall be:

a.   On *net capital gain* - a capital gains tax rate of 20% (**reduced from 28% effective on or after May 7, 1997**), or

b.   (Effective on or after May 7, 1997) for taxpayer's in the 15% tax bracket - a 10% capital gains tax rate is imposed.

115

Note:
*   The "Act of 1997" for capital gains is effective for qualified transactions on or after May 7, 1997.

*   The holding period to qualify for capital gains treatment was lengthened to 18 months from 12 months, effective July 29, 1997.

Historically Capital Gains have been treated differently than ordinary income. Typically, this "preference has been expressed in the form of a lower rate applicable to long-term gain. In taxable years for Capital Gains and losses realized and recognized after May 7, 1997, the preference has become much more complex than it had been previously.

To benefit under the new system, a taxpayer must have a *net capital gain (i.e., an excess of long-term capital gain over net short capital loss). Absent a net capital gain, the taxpayer whether corporation or individual, is in effect taxed on short-term capital gains at the same rates as on ordinary income.*

As before, the deduction of capital losses is limited. In the case of corporate taxpayers, a limitation in capital gains realized in the same taxable year. Excess losses may be carried back for three years and forward for five years. But after that they expire. Losses are deductible to the extent of capital gains realized in the same taxable year, but up to $3,000 of "excess" losses may be deducted currently. If the individual taxpayer still has losses, these may be carried forward indefinitely until used up.

Despite sweeping changes in 1997, generally favorable to taxpayers, corporate taxpayers have no capital gains preference, even for long-term capital gains realized and recognized after May 7, 1997. However, for individual taxpayers it is a different story, albeit a very complex one. For a taxpayer who has *net capital gain,* realized and recognized after the 1997 changes, it is no longer possible to state easily that a flat rate of 20, 25 or 30 percent applies to the net capital gain rather than the taxpayer's rate on his/her ordinary income. The taxpayer's liability for net capital gain consists, therefore of the sum of the following:

(1) 28% - for gains attributable to "collectible" (§§1(h)(5)(A)(i)) and to the sale or exchange of "section 1201" stock (§§1(h)(5)(A)(ii));

(2) 25% - for the excess, if any, of

(i) "unrecaptured" IRC §1250 gain (i.e. the gain on "section 1250 property" which would have been treated as ordinary income if IRC §1250 recaptured all gains and not just those attributable to accelerated depreciation over

(ii) modified taxable income

(3) 20% of the adjusted net capital gain (net capital gains with adjustments) IRC §1(h)(4)

(4) 10% (an 8% rate is possible) on certain five-year gain IRC §1(h)(2)(A)

For taxpayers who sell their principal residence on or after May 7, 1997, the former system which permitted the gain realized by the taxpayer on the transaction to be "rolled over" (IRC §1034 or to be excluded) (maximum exclusion - $125,000 under IRC §121), has been supplanted by a provision that is, it seems, both more and less general than the provision it replaced. The relatively new provision more than doubles from $125,000 to $500,000. To qualify for the $500,000 limitation, the statute requires that:

(1) both spouses use and occupy the residence as their principal residence, which is owned by at least one of the spouses, for at least two of the five years immediately preceding the year in which the sale or exchange takes place;

(2) a husband and wife file a joint return; and

(3) neither spouse is ineligible for the exclusion because similar benefits were provided within the two years immediately preceding the sale or exchange, except where the move was connected with the commencement of work at a new location.

* Beginning in 2001 a new maximum rate of 18% takes effect for assets purchased after 2000 and held for at least five years. Gains on sales of collectibles continues to be taxed at a rate of 28%.

* Under "The Act of 1997" the tax rate on *certain depreciable real property* = 25%

10. Using Deductions, Exemptions, Dependents and the Earned Income Credit

* Deductions reduce the amount of Taxable Income while a credit reduces the amount of taxes that must be paid.

* Deductions are presumed not to be allowed unless the code specifically permits it.

* Limited items of a personal nature are deductible even though they have no connection to business. See, generally, IRC §§ 163 (relating to interest), 164 (relating to taxes), 165 (relating to certain losses of the taxpayer) and 212 (relating to expenses incurred by the taxpayer in either income producing or in maintaining income producing property or for tax advise).

* Allowable deductions are classified "above-the-line" (i.e., they are taken into account in determining the taxpayer's AGI (IRC § 62)) or they are "below-the-line (i.e., the taxpayer must "itemize" such deductions (IRC § 63(d))).

    a. Deductions from GI or "Above-the-line"

        i. Trade and business deductions (IRC § 62(a)(1)), except trade and business deductions of employees

        ii. Reimbursed expenses of employees (e.g., travel and transportation expenses, union dues) The reimbursement is included in income and the expense is deducted from AGI (IRC § 62(a)(2)A). If employee is required to account precisely for reimbursed expense, taxpayer is permitted to exclude both the reimbursement from income and the expense from deduction.

        iii. Deduction for capital losses or other losses from the sale and exchange of property IRC § 62(a)(3)(4)), if capitalized, may not be fully deductible (IRC § 1211).

        iv. Expenses deductible under IRC § 212: Rent and Royalties only.

        v. Alimony (IRC § 61(a)(10).

        vi. Moving Expenses under IRC § 217 , IRC § 62(a)(5).

        vii. Includes cash reimbursements to the extent that the employee would have been entitled to a moving deduction had he paid it himself. (IRC § 217)

b. Distinction - almost always preferable to have deductions from GI (above-the-line) than from AGI (below-the-line) because:

  i. below must be greater than a standard deduction
  Standard Deduction: a substitute for deducting "below-the-line" deductions. Taxpayer is entitled to the *larger* of itemized deductions or the standard deduction.

  A) Amount: Standard is $6,700 on a joint return, 5,900 for the head of the household, 4,000 for singles and 3,350 for married persons filing separately. These amounts are adjusted for inflation.

  B) Elderly and Blind: $600 additional for married elderly and $150 for single older than 65 years.

  C) Dependents: if TP is taken as a dependent on another return the standard deduction is limited to the individuals earned income, or $500, whatever is greater. (no personal exemption if claimed by another)

  ii. Medical Expenses: reduced by 7.5% of the taxpayer's AGI; therefore the lower the AGI the more medical expenses allowable.

  iii. Child Care Credit: is greater if AGI is lower

  iv. Charitable contributions limitations are based on a percentage of AGI. Therefore, the higher the AGI the more charitable contributions are allowed
  Charitable Contributions: TP's are entitled to a deduction for contributions to recognized charities, operated predominantly for charitable, religious, scientific, literary or educational purposes. (IRC § 170(c))

  A) Limitations:

    1) Individual: up to 50% AGI

      a) carry-over if contribution exceeds 50% of TP's contribution base. TP can carry-over for the next 5 years

      b) Corporations: 10% of taxable income and carry-over

      c) Substantiation Requirement if the contribution is greater than $250 with written acknowledgment and receipt.

2) Gifts in Kind: TP may deduct FMV to a 30% limitation of AGI if the gift in kind is a capital appreciation property.
3) No Deduction if TP benefits from the contribution. The contribution needs to be detached and disinterested (*Duberstein*) to be deducted with no identifiable benefit (*Hernandez*).

c. Personal Exemptions

General rule :
i. exemption for individual TP; and
ii. exemptions if joint

IRC § 151 Allowance for deductions for personal exemptions

IRC § 151(d) Exemption amount = $2,000 (adjusted for inflation) can be taken out only once in a year.

IRC § 151(b) Exemptions allowed:
i. for an individual return = deduction allowed
ii. If married and filing jointly = 2 deductions

IRC § 151(a) Exemption allowed for dependent if TP provides one-half of support of the dependent.
* Additional exemption for each dependent is allowed.

IRC § 151(c) Exemption allowed for each dependent must satisfy the relationship test: IRC § 151(b) dependent is a close relative or has a disability and lives in abode with TP.

IRC § 151(c) Exemption provided if GI of dependent is less than exemption amount and if dependent is younger than 19 or a student under 24 at years' end attending an IRC § 170 institution or pursues a full-time course of on-farm training under an accredited agent (IRC § 151(c)(4)).

IRC § 151(c)(2) Exemption is denied if a dependent is married and files a joint return.

IRC § 151(c)(3) Defines child or step as allowed for exemption.

IRC § 151(c)(5) In calculating GI of a handicapped dependent do not include services performed at an accredited workshop where medical care is furnished there and the income arises solely from the workshop.

IRC § 151(d)(3) Phaseout
Personal exemptions are phased out at a rate of 2% for every $2,500 that the taxpayer's AGI exceeds the threshold amount. ($1250 for married individuals filing separately).

IRC § 151(d)(3)(C) Threshold Amount = $150,000 for a joint return or surviving spouse, $125,000 for a head of household, $100,000 for an individual who is neither married, a surviving spouse nor a head of household, $75,000 for a married individual filing separately.

IRC § 151(d)(4) Adjustment for Inflation for every year after 1989, the dollar amount ($2,500) and for every year after 1991, the threshold amount shall be increased by the amount multiplied by the cost of living adjustment as determined under IRC § 1(f)(3).
* below-the-line deduction, but not subject to 2% floor on miscellaneous itemized deductions or phaseout.

d. Dependents

IRC § 152 Dependent defined

A dependent is a person who derives half of its support from the taxpayer and is related to the taxpayer by blood, marriage or adoption in any way specified below, or who meets special requirements:
  Requirements:
  i. Son or daughter of the taxpayer or a descendant of either, stepson or stepdaughter, brother, sister, father, mother or either's ancestors; **stepparent**, son or daughter of brother or sister; son, daughter, mother, father, brother, or **sister-in-law**; or
  ii. Any individual (other than one who was a spouse at any time during the year under IRC § 7703) who has his principal place of residence at the taxpayer's house and is a member of his family.

Note:

* Exemptions are not subjected to the 2% floor on miscellaneous items or the deduction phaseout. IRC § 67 (take this + standard)
* In determining whether the taxpayer supplied over one-half of the dependent's support items provided in kind. Housing, food, and others are included, but services provided to the dependent are not.
* Any scholarship received by a dependent is not considered when determining whether one provides one-half of the dependent's support.
* In divorced families the exemption is given to the person who has custody for the majority of the year, regardless of who pays the support or upkeep.

e.   The Tax Credit

A tax credit is not a deduction. A tax credit is a direct offset to the tax otherwise due.

Provides a dollar for dollar credit to the tax liability.

i.   Earned Income Credit
IRC § 32 Earned income credit

IRC § 32(a)(1): Gives credit (to apply after the tax liability is computed) equal to a % of TP earned income.

IRC § 32 (a)(2): If TP's AGI goes too high, the credit is phased out. This provision is a substitution for working low-income people.

The amount of credit for a TP with 1 qualifying child :
With a child younger than 19 years or a full-time student less than 24 years of age, the credit is 34% if TP earned income up to $6,000.
Phaseout: the amount is reduced by 15.98% of earned income of $11,000.

ii. Household Expenses and Dependent Care

IRC § 21 Expenses for household and dependent care necessary for gainful employment

IRC § 21(a) If an individual maintains a household with qualified dependents, a percentage of the amount spent on services is used as a credit against taxes owed.

If TP's AGI rises above $10,000, the credit phases down from 30% to 20% by 1% for each $2,000 (or fraction thereof) of the taxpayer's AGI, but never goes below 20%.

IRC § 21(b)(1) Qualified Individual = (i) child under 13, (ii) dependent who is physically or mentally incapable of taking care of himself, or (iii) spouse who can't take care of himself.

IRC § 21(b)(2) Employment related expenses = household services, care of dependent
*   Does not include overnight camp
*   Outside of the home centers must comply with all regulations, must receive a fee, and must care for more than six individuals Maximum amount of expenses that may be taken into account are limited to $2,400 for one dependent and $4,800 for two dependents or more

Formula:
 (Credit = Applicable Percentage)
                        X
(TP Employment related expenses)

Max Credit = 30% X $2,400 = $720

The credit cannot exceed the earned income of the spouse making the least amount of money.

No credits for payments made to related individuals if they are allowed as a deduction for the taxable year, or if made to a child of the taxpayer
*   Must include name and address of the provider in the tax return
*   Divorced parent can take the credit, even if he can't take the exemption
*   A person maintains a household if he pays for over 50% of the expenses for the year

Example 1:
Sue is single. Her AGI is $100,000. Sue spends $20,000 on day care for one child.
    Credit = 20% X 2,400 = $480

Example 1:
Sue is married and made $100,000.
Her spouse made $2,000.
IRC § 21(d)(1)(b) applies, therefore the
lesser of the married couples earned income
is the limit for employment related expenses.
Credit = 20% X 2,000 = $400

Smith v. Comm'r, 113 F.2d 114 (2d Cir. 1940)
New phenomenon, wife works outside the house.
Held: That this is not a deductible expense.
IRC § 21 now overrules this.

VI. PROPERTY TRANSACTIONS

When a taxpayer holds property which either appreciates or depreciates in value, the fluctuation is without tax consequence until the taxpayer sells, exchanges or otherwise disposes of the property for money and/or other property. If the taxpayer has realized a gain on the transaction, measured by comparing his investment in the asset (referred to as "Adjusted Basis') and the value of what the taxpayer has received on the transaction (the "Amount Realized"), the gain will be characterized and then subjected to tax according to this characterization. Losses are similarly treated, except that they generally produce deductions which lower tax rather than produce additional tax liability.

This chapter and the one that follows will focus on the characterization of the gain or loss **realized and recognized** by the taxpayer on a sale, exchange or on the disposition of property.

As a starting point, two fundamental principles must be considered:
1. It is necessary to have a gain or loss which has been **realized and recognized** *before* it can be **characterized;** and
2. Only **capital assets** which have been **sold or exchanged** can produce **capital gain or loss.**

A. IRC § 1221 CAPITAL ASSETS DEFINED

Section 532(a) of the Tax Relief Extension Act of 1999 has added an important limitation to the statutory scheme which defines a capital asset. A capital asset is essentially all of a taxpayer's property, subject to specific statutory limitations. The statute has been amended by § 532 of the Tax Relief Extension Act.

1. §1221. Capital asset defined.

IRC §1221 as amended now reads as follows:

*(a) **In general.** For purposes of this subtitle, the term "capital asset" means property held by the taxpayer (whether or not connected with his trade or business), but does not include:*

(1) stock in trade of the taxpayer or other property of a kind which would properly be included in the inventory of the taxpayer if on hand at the close of the taxable year, or property held by the taxpayer primarily for sale to customers in the ordinary course of his trade or business.

(2) property, used in his trade or business, of a character which is subject to the allowance for depreciation provided in section 167, or real property used in his trade or business;

(3) a copyright, a literary, musical, or artistic composition, a letter or memorandum or similar property, held by:

> *(A) a taxpayer whose personal efforts created such property;*

> *(B) in the case of a letter, memorandum, or similar property, a taxpayer for whom such property was prepared or produced; or*

> *(C) a taxpayer in whose hands the basis of such property is determined, for purposes of determining gain from a sale or exchange, in whole or in part by reference to the basis of such property in the hands of a taxpayer described in subparagraph (A) and (B).*

(4) accounts or notes receivable acquired in the ordinary course of trade or business for services rendered or from the sale of property described in paragraph (1).

(5) a publication of the United States Government (including Congressional Record) which is received from the United States Government or any agency thereof, other than by purchase at the price at which it is offered for sale to the public, and which is held by:

> *(A) a taxpayer who received such publication; or*

> *(B) a taxpayer in whose hands the basis of such publication is determined, for purposes of determining gain from a sale or exchange, in whole or in part by reference to the basis of such publication in the hands of a taxpayer described in subparagraph (i); [and]*

(6) any commodities derivative financial instrument held by a commodities derivatives dealer, unless:

> *(A) it is established to the satisfaction of the Secretary that such instrument has no connection to the activities of such dealer as a dealer; and*

(B) such instrument is clearly identified in such dealer's records as being described in subparagraph (i) before the close of the day on which it was acquired, originated, or entered into (or such other time as the Secretary may by regulations prescribe);

(7) any hedging transaction which is clearly identified as such before the close of the day on which it was acquired, originated, or entered into (or such other time as the Secretary may by regulations prescribe); or

(8) supplies of a type regularly used or consumed by the taxpayer in the ordinary course of a trade or business of the taxpayer.

(b) **Definitions and special rules**

(1) Commodities derivative financial instruments. For purposes of subsection (a)(6):

(A) Commodities derivatives dealer. The term "commodities derivatives dealer" means a person which regularly offers to enter into, assume, offset, assign, or terminate positions in commodities derivative financial instruments with customers in the ordinary course of a trade or business.

(B) Specified index. The term "specified index" means any one or more or a combination of:

(i) In general. The term "commodities derivative financial instrument" means any contract or financial instrument with respect to commodities (other than a share of stock in a corporation, a beneficial interest in a partnership or trust, a note, bond, debenture, or other evidence of indebtedness, or a section 1256 contract (as defined in section 1256(b)), the value or settlement price of which is calculated by or determined by reference to a specified index.

(ii) Specified index. The term "specified index" means any one or more or any combination of:

(I) a fixed rate, price, or amount; or

(II) a variable rate, price, or amount, which is based on any current objectively determinable financial or economic information with respect to commodities which is not

within the control of any of the parties to the contract or
instrument and is not unique to any of the parties'
circumstances.

(2) Hedging transaction:

*(A) in general. For purposes of this section, the term "hedging
transaction" means any transaction entered into by the taxpayer in
the normal course of the taxpayer's trade or business, primarily:*

*(i) to manage risk of price changes or currency fluctuations with
respect to ordinary property which is held or to be held by the
taxpayer;*

*(ii) to manage risk of interest rate or price changes or currency
fluctuations with respect to borrowings made or to be made, or
ordinary obligations incurred or to be incurred, by the taxpayer;
or*

*(iii) to manage such other risks as the Secretary may prescribe
in regulations.*

*(B) Treatment of nonidentification or improper identification of
hedging transaction. Notwithstanding subsection (a)(7), the
Secretary shall prescribe regulation to properly characterize any
income, gain, expense or loss arising from a transaction:*

*(i) which is hedging transaction but which was not identified as
such in accordance with subsection (a)(7); or*

(ii) which was so identified but is not a hedging transaction.

*(3) Regulations. The Secretary shall prescribe such regulations as are
appropriate to carry out the purposes of paragraphs (6) and (7) of
subsection (a) in the case of transactions involving related parties.*

2. Property used in the trade or business & involuntary conversions
    (Quasi-capital assets): **IRC § 1231.**

Under certain very specific circumstances, the statute permits taxpayers
to in effect have the best of all possible words (i.e. capital gains -- if the
net result of his/her Section 1231 transaction is a gain -- and ordinary

losses -- if the net result is a loss). To qualify for IRC § 1231, the TP must either sell/exchange property:

    i.   which is held for more than a year and is used in the taxpayer's trade or business; or

    ii. suffer an involuntary conversion with respect to certain business and/or capital gains property that is held for a long-term (more than one year) and is involuntarily converted.

The operation of IRC § 1231 is basically very simple:

    a. **Hodgepot No. 1:** TP is required to isolate all of his gains and losses derived from property that is not a "pure" capital asset within IRC § 1221 principally due to IRC §1221(2).* A similar quarantining process is required for gains and losses incurred in "involuntary conversions" of both "pure" capital assets under IRC §1221 and of "property used in the trade or business" within IRC §1231.

NOTE: If the net result of Hodgepot No. 1 is that the gains exceed losses, <u>all</u> of the transactions are considered with the remaining transactions identified in subparagraph "b" below. In contrast, if the gains fail to exceed losses -- i.e. losses equal to or exceed gains -- each gain and each loss is treated as ordinary gain or ordinary loss, as the case may be.

    b. **Hodgepot No. 2:** This next step also involves a netting process similar to that in subparagraph "a" above. It requires that TP add up or net his gains and/or losses from the sale or exchange of Section 1231 property, including the net amount of gains and losses from Hodgepot No. 1.

    c. This next step is a two-prong process:

        i.   Consider the net value of the involuntary conversions -- i.e. whether the total gains equal or exceed the amount of losses derived from involuntary conversion; and

---

* "IRC § 1231 Property" includes property identified in IRS § 1221(2). That is, depreciable property used in TP's trade or business or real property used in suor business. It does not include, however, inventory or other property held for sale in the ordinary course of TP's trade or business.

      ii.   If the answer to subparagraph "i" above is yes, each of the involuntary conversions is considered along with "pure" capital assets.

IRC §1231 provides an additional source of capital gains and losses.

IRC §1231(a)(1) If IRC § 1231 gains are greater than IRC § 1231 losses then all transactions are treated as long-term capital gains/losses.

IRC §1231(a)(2) If IRC § 1231 gains are less than IRC 1231 losses, all of the gains and all of the losses are not capital gains/losses but ordinary gains and losses.

IRC §1231(a)(3) Gain/loss = sale or exchange on property used in the taxpayer's trade or business and compulsory or involuntary conversion (destruction, theft, etc.) into money or other property of long-term capital assets or property used in the trade or business.

IRC §1231(a)(3)(b) Property used in the ordinary conduct of the taxpayer's business = machinery and other long-term depreciable property under IRC § 167. This does not include inventory, property held for sale to customers, copyrights (see IRC § 1221).
Land, buildings, & machinery are fixed depreciable business assets.

IRC § 1231(c) If the taxpayer had a net gain on IRC § 1231 assets but had net IRC § 1231 losses in the preceding five years, the gain will be treated as ordinary income to the extent of unrecaptured losses.

Net Gains = LT Cap gain

Net Loss = Ordinary Losses

Van Suetendale v. Comm'r, 3 T.C.M. 987 (1944), aff'd, 152 F. 2d 654 (2d Cir. 1945).
A dealer in securities, wanted to treat securities as non-capital assets. Stocks are traditionally treated as capital assets, but the dealer contends that the stocks are inventory for him since he was a dealer. However, he failed to produce evidence to distinguish between his sales as a dealer and those as a trader, investor, or speculator.
Held: Securities were not inventory. Taxpayer was buying and selling them for his own benefit, as an investor. Consequently, they were properly treated as capital assets.

Biedenharn Realty v. U.S., 526 F. 2d 409 (5th Cir.), *cert. den'd.* 429 U.S. 819 (1976).
A family formed a corporation to hold family assets. They purchased a plantation for $50,000. Initially it was meant to be an investment. Later, however, they sold the plantation in many individual lots for $800,000. The taxpayer wanted to treat the gain as capital gain. However, the IRS argued that gains or losses were ordinary since the corporation was acting as a "dealer" in selling to customers.
Held: Gains were ordinary not capital, the court looked at purpose/ motive of the sale, not the purchase. Had taxpayer sold to a developer who then divided it up, it would still be a capital investment in the hands of investors. This was different.

Further, the Court looked at the following factors to determine whether the sale was within IRC § 1221:
  i.   frequency of sales
  ii. improvements made to the property
  iii. solicitations and advertising
  iv. brokerage activities
  v.   use of business office to promote sales
  vi. character and degree of supervision by taxpayer of the sales representative
  vii. time or effort devoted to sales

Practical Application:
Look at the continuity and number of sales, the improvements made to the property or subdivisions made, purpose for which purchased.
Here, there was a steady flow of sales, substantial improvements made, and although originally intended as an investment the purpose changed.

Corn Products Refining v. Comm'r, 350 U.S. 46 (1955).
Manufacturer of corn products bought corn futures (contract for future delivery) to protect its supply of corn. It sold some of the futures at a profit which it sought to treat as capital gain. But the IRS successfully claimed that the corn futures were purchased for sale in the ordinary course of the TP's regular trade or business. Thus, the futures were more like inventory than an investment. Therefore, should be ordinary gain.
Held: Gain should be treated as ordinary income, not capital gain.

Arkansas Best v. Comm'r, 485 U.S. 212 (1988)
A diversified holding company purchased 65% of a bank and claimed that it purchased the stock as business inventory. The bank went into

foreclosure when the real estate market declined. The holding company sold the bank stock and claimed the loss as an ordinary loss. The IRS claimed that this was a capital loss not an ordinary loss.

Held: The loss was a capital loss, statute says what it means and means what it says. Do not look so much to the context in which the gain or loss was realized and recognized, but into the plain meaning and intent of the statute as indicated by its specific language. Here the asset sold or exchanged was stock in a bank. Absent special circumstances, stock is a capital asset, unless TP is a "dealer" who holds the stock for sale in the ordinary course of its trade or business.

Rule:

Gain or loss from the sale of commodity futures contracts that are an integral part of the business inventory purchasing falls under the inventory exception of IRC § 1221(1). Therefore, it is not treated as a capital asset. Consequently, neither capital gain nor capital asset is a possibility.

Hedging = Insurance = Ordinary loss
Speculation = investment = capital gain/loss

3. Gain from dispositions of certain depreciable property (ordinary income + CG) IRC § 1245

When depreciable property is sold for an amount above the adjusted basis, the gain thus realized is treated as ordinary income to the extent of prior deductions and any amount left over will likely be treated as a capital gain under IRC § 1231.

Recapture of Depreciation: To the extent gain does not exceed depreciation, it is "recaptured" and treated as ordinary income and not as capital gain.

IRC § 1231 and IRC § 1245 characterize the gain not losses. If property is not sold at a gain, there is no recapture.

4. Gain from dispositions of certain depreciable realty: IRC § 1250

Before: IRC § 1245 and IRC § 1250 were enacted, gain attributable to depreciation was capital gain.

Note: Under the "1997 Act," a portion of the "certain real property gain" that would otherwise be fixed at capital gains tax rates (20%

maximum for gains attributable to transactions on or after May 7, 1997) will, nonetheless, be subject to tax at 28%. IRC § 1(h)(7).

Example 1:
Taxpayer buys machines for use in his trade or business. He pays $10,000 for the machines and properly depreciates them by $4,000. His basis in the machines accordingly declines to $6,000. He sells the machines for $9,000. Although the transaction produces a gain for the taxpayer [Amount Realized - $9,000 minus adjusted Basis = $6,000 = $3,000 Gain Realized and Recognized], it is almost immediately clear that all of this gain is attributable to the depreciation deductions. Had they not been taken, the taxpayer's basis would have remained at $10,000 and a loss of $1,000 would have been produced. IRC § 1245 "recaptures" this "depreciation gain" and converts it to ordinary income rather than capital gain.

Example 2:
The same facts as in the previous example except that the value of the machines actually increases to $11,000 while used by the taxpayer. At this point, the taxpayer sells the machines. Here, the taxpayer has a gain of $5,000 [$11,000 *minus* $6,000 = $5,000]. However, assuming the sale would otherwise produce a long-term capital gain, only $4,000, the difference between the taxpayer's basis ($6,000) and the "recomputed basis" [Adjusted Basis ($6,000) + Depreciation allowed or Allowable ($4,000) = $10,000] represents gain attributable to depreciation deductions. The balance of the gain, $1,000, represents appreciation in the nature of the asset and can properly be characterized as capital gain.

5.   Exchange of property held for productive use or investment IRC § 1031

IRC § 1031(a) Nonrecognition of gain or loss from exchanges solely in Kind

IRC § 1031(a)(1) No gain or loss shall be recognized from like kind exchanges of property held for productive use in a trade or business or for investment
Four requirements to be satisfied to have like kind exchange:
   a.   exchange of property
   b.   property given must be in trade, business or investment
   c.   property exchanged must be like kind

  d. property received must be used in trade, business or investment

Reg § 1.031(a)-1(b) like kind = The general nature or character of the property, not grade or quality

Example 1:
A owns a house and B owns a car. They make an exchange. This is a realization event (Cottage Savings v. Comm'r., 499 U.S. 534 (1991)) and the amount of appreciation gets taxed. Houses (real property) and cars (personal property) are NOT property of like kind.

A's house: FMV = 100% Basis = $ 30
B's car   : FMV = 100% Basis = $150

The amount realized is the value of the property received, and basis is that which is exchanged away (Substituted Basis)

Therefore:
A: Amount realized = value of the car = $100
    Basis = house basis   = $ 30
    GAIN = $ 70

Note:
B realized a loss of $50 on the exchange. The loss is determined by comparing the "amount realized" by B (fair market value of A's house equal to $100) compared to B's basis in his car $150. IRC § 1001(a) and (b).

Example 2:
A owns Blackacre and B owns Yellowacre, and they exchange properties.

Blackacre : FMV = 100, Basis = $ 30
Yellowacre: FMV = 100, Basis = $150

Assuming that Blackacre and Yellowacre are properties "of like kind" congress has decided as a matter of tax policy that this is not an appropriate time to tax, even though there is a realization event. The property exchanged is too similar. The gain or loss is not yet recognized

IRC § 1031(a)(2) Exceptions: "nonrecognition" not applicable to stocks, bonds or notes, inventory or other items held for sale, securities of indebtedness or interest, partnership interests, certificates in trust or legal rights in an action and services.

IRC § 1031(a)(3)(A) Deferred exchange.
Property must be identified within 45 days after the date on which the taxpayer transfers the property, and

Reg § 1.031(k) Property must be received within 180 days of the transfer of the taxpayer's property or the due date of the transferor's tax return if that is earlier.

Starker v. U.S., 602 F. 2nd 1341 (9th Cir. 1979).
Relatives entered into a like kind exchange agreement. Corporation wanted land to cut down the trees for tax reasons. Starker wanted to exchange it for different land. Corporation wanted the land now, Starker wanted it in 5 years.
Held: That the property received within 5 years of a transaction in exchange for property relinquished is considered a like kind exchange for the purposes of non-recognition.
This has since been overruled.

Today, property must be identified within 45 days and exchange is to be completed not more than 180 days after transfer of the exchanged property under IRC § 1031(a)(3), in order to be considered a like kind exchange.

IRC § 1031(b) Boot = property not "of a like kind" exchanged in conjunction with like kind property.

IRC § 1031(e) Livestock of different sexes are not like kind property.

Realized gain = FMV of relinquished property minus the adjusted basis of the relinquished property.

* If there is gain in an exchange with boot then the taxpayer will recognize the gain to the extent that it equals the boot. Recognize the lesser of gain realized and the value of the boot. Never recognize more than realized gain.

IRC § 1031(c) If there is a realized loss, and boot is received, then the loss is, nonetheless not recognized (IRC § 1031 (c)).

IRC § 1031(d) Basis: New Basis = Old Basis *plus* Gain Recognized *minus* loss recognized and any money received.

If **no boot is received,** then the Basis of the property on the exchange (new property) = Basis of the property relinquished (old property).

Cash Boot Paid: Basis = relinquished property Basis *plus* amount of cash boot paid.

Basis of Boot Property Received = Boot's FMV

Paid Boot = Payor's property received Basis = Boot FMV *plus* property relinquished Basis

Example:
A owns Blackacre: FMV = 100, Basis = $ 30;
B owns Yellowacre: FMV = $80, Basis = $150

A and B exchange properties. A also receives $20 from B to equalize the exchange:

On the exchange, A realizes a gain of $70 (value of property received minus $80 plus cash of $20 = $100; basis = $30; gain realized = $70). Of the $70 gain realized, the "boot", of $20 requires gain recognition in that amount. IRC § 1031(b).

A's basis in the new property is $30, determined as follows:
  i.   basis in the old property ($30)
  ii. less cash received ($20)
  iii. increased by gain recognized ($20)
  iv. new basis ($30)

Note:
* Recognize Boot gain difference between the FMV and Basis.
* Must recognize the gain realized where boot is received, but receipt of boot does not compel loss recognition.
* "Like kind" refers to the general character or nature of the property, rather than its grade or quality. A parking lot and a high-rise apartment building are therefore "of a like kind," despite the obvious differences between them. Real property is like real property and personal property is like personal property. Thus, a parking lot is like an apartment building.
* Real property within the US is not of a like kind with real property outside of the US.

* No loss is recognized with like kind exchanges IRC § 1031(a)(1), even though Boot may be received. Payoff of Boot increases his/her basis in property relinquished in the exchange by the amount of cash Boot paid or the basis of property boot surrendered. In determining the basis of the new property received, the payor's basis in the property surrendered includes the amount cash paid or basis of boot property surrounded to the other party to the exchange as indicated.

* Definition of like kind is stricter with personal property than it is with real property. A ranch and a hotel may be like kind, but gold and silver cubes are not. (Rev. Rul. 82-166, 1982 C.B. 190 and §1031). In a pure like kind exchange, gain/loss realized will be recognized only upon a subsequent disposition of the property received by the taxpayer.

* IRC § 1031 is an automatic exception to IRC § 1001. Apart from structure, it is not elective at the option of the parties. However, if a taxpayer wants to recognize a gain or a loss in the context of what would otherwise be a qualifying like kind exchange, structural changes to the transaction must be implemented. For example, if TP wishes to recognize a gain, he/she will have to arrange for some sort of boot (cash or non-like kind property) to be received by TP. This will cause realized gain to be recognized, but not in excess of the amount of the boot.

* If the TP wishes to recognize a loss, IRC § 1031(c) must be dealt with. Typically, this involves a sale of the loss asset to an unrelated third party in a transaction that takes place prior to and separate from the like kind exchange.

* **CAUTION:** The mere fact that the sale occurs prior to the like kind exchange does not insulate it from scrutiny and the possibility of its inclusion as part of the exchange. Factors that the IRS considers includes: 1) the time interval between third party sale and like kind exchange; 2) the relationship of the parties; 3) whether the asset is sold for its FMV or not; 4) any side agreements or other restrictions imposed on the purchaser of the loss property which might tend to indicate the purchaser's continuing interest in the property.

* Transaction which would otherwise qualify as being exclusively of a "like kind" will frequently involve the receipt of boot property. Boot is property that is not of a like kind with the property exchanged by the taxpayer. As for example, where the TP has an expiring net operating loss available which would shelter the gain thus recognized.

* Rules regarding like kind exchanges can be concisely summarized as follows:

No Boot	Merely a technical realization of gain/loss. Gain/loss has been realized, but will not be recognized. Thus, there is no current recognition and any gain/loss realized will be recognized only upon subsequent disposition in a taxable transaction. Gain/loss realized will be preserved to adjustments to TP's basis in property received.
Cash Boot Paid by TP	Basis increase to the extent of the cash boot so that gain is not taxed twice. Cash boot paid increases TP's basis and therefore reduces gain or increases loss.
Noncash Boot Paid By TP	When boot property is paid by TP, it is treated as a separate taxable transaction occurring simultaneously with the non-taxable transaction. Thus, gain/loss on the boot property is possible.
Cash/Property Boot Received by TP	Receipt of boot, whether in the form of cash or "other property," causes realized gain to be recognized, but not realized losses. TP's basis in boot property is equal to its FMV.

Gain = Value of Boot

Jordan Marsh v. Comm'r, 269 F. 2d 453 (2d Cir 1959).

Property sold for a lesser price and then leased back on a long-term basis.

Held: That this is not a like kind exchange therefore not applicable to IRC § 1031.

If the sale is considered separate from the lease, then any loss or gain is recognized.

Taxpayer cashed out investment and therefore a loss was recognized.

Rev. Rul. § 56-437, 1956-2 C.B. 507

Converting a joint tenancy to a tenancy in common is a nontaxable transaction for income tax purposes.

There is no sale or exchange of property, nor is there a taxable gain or a deductible loss.

Rev. Rul. § 79-44, 1979-1 C.B. 265
Converting tenants in common in two jointly owned parcels into
individually owned parcels is a nontaxable partition under IRC §
1001(a). However, since the property was like kind IRC § 1031 applies.
Since one party received the parcel with a note from the other, that party
received boot and will need to recognize any gain in excess of the FMV
of the boot.

6.   Rollover of gain on sale of principal residence: IRC § 1034

**Approved legislation under the Tax Relief Act of 1997 for
Capital Gains is effective May 7, 1997:**
Married couples filing jointly are able to exclude as much as $500,000
of profit realized on the sale of a principal residence, even if the
taxpayers opt not to "ROLLOVER" the gain to a new principal
residence. Singles can exclude as much as $250,000.

Note: It is important to note that the Tax Relief Act of 1997 new
legislation replaces IRC §§ 1034 (the rollover provision) and 121 (the
one-time exclusion of $125,000 on a gain for taxpayers who have
attained the age of 55).

The hidden trap? All gain in excess of $500,000 is subject to tax,
even if the taxpayer purchases another principal residence that costs as
much as the old residence was sold for.

To be eligible for the full exclusion under the "Tax Relief Act",
homeowners typically would have to occupy their home at least two
years during the five years prior to the sale.

The full exclusion is available once every two years.

**Sales or exchanges of principal residence prior to May 7,
1997**. Prior to the 1997 Act, a generous exclusion was available for
taxpayers who realized gain from the sale or exchange of a principal
residence. Those TPs who reinvested ("rolled over") the proceeds of sale
into a new principal residence which cost as much as the old, no gain
was recognized in the year in which the sale or exchange occurred.

When a taxpayer sells their personal residence and realizes a gain in
excess of the exclusion allowed for capital gains on sales of primary
residence, the recognition of the gain may be deferred, if the taxpayer
"rolls over" the gain into a new personal residence within the time period

specified in IRC § 1034 (within two years before or after the sale or exchange of the old residence).

Notice: of *new tax developments* as of July 10, **1998**: Proposed changes effective upon the President signing into law. The Capital gains tax change would be effective retroactive for all sales as of January 1, 1998.

Change effects the homeowner.
If a home owner sells a home owned for less than two years, the homeowner will be allowed partial relief based on a fraction rather than the owners actual profit.
For example:
If a single taxpayer homeowner makes $125,000 profit by selling his/her home owned for less than one year, that taxpayer would be allowed to exclude the entire $125,000 profit (gain), not just half the profit.

The hidden trap: This could mean higher taxes for homeowners who have *huge* short-term profits.

IRC § 1034(a) Nonrecognition of gain: If property used as the taxpayer's principal residence is sold and a new one is purchased within a period of two years before or after the sale, where the "Adjusted Sales Price" of the old house is less than the cost of the new house, the gain will not be recognized.

IRC § 1034(a) A gain will be recognized where the "Adjusted Sales Price" of the old house is greater than the cost of the new house.

Gain = Adjusted Sales Price - Cost of new property

IRC § 1034(b)(1) Adjusted Sale Price: Amount realized minus the expense for work performed on the old house to assist in the sale.

IRC § 1034(b)(2) Limitations: The reduction referred to in IRC § 1034(b)(1) applies only to expenses.

IRC § 1034(b)(2)(A) Work performed during the 90 day period ending on the day when the contract to sell the old house is entered into.

IRC § 1034(b)(2)(B) which are paid for on or before the 30th day after the date of the sale.

IRC § 1034(b)(2)(C) which are not allowable as IRC § 63 deductions and not taken into account when computing the amount realized from the sale of the old house.

IRC § 1034(e) Basis of New Residence: Basis of the new residence is decreased by the amount of gain not recognized under IRC § 1034(a).

IRC § 1034(f) Stock in a co-op is eligible to be considered principal residence for the purpose of this section as long as the apartment is used by both the buyer and the seller as a principal residence.

Basis = cost of the new residence less the gain on the sale of the old residence that was not recognized.

Examples: Under IRC § 1034, § 121 and "The Act of 1997":

Under IRC § 1034
(1) Buy home for $100,000 hold it for 5 years and sell it for $150,000. Gain is $50,000, which can be *entirely* excluded if TP reinvests in new principal residence within the 2 year time limit.

Under IRC § 121
(2) Same as (1), except no reinvestment, but one of the married sellers has reached the age of 55. *All* of gain is excluded under one-time election under IRC § 121 (up to maximum of $125,000 of gain).

The new rules are seemingly more generous. And in most cases, they are, *but* there are traps for the unwary.

(3) Same facts as (1); same result under the new Act which *does not* require reinvestment.

(4) Same facts as (2); same result under new Act, but *not* limited to one-time election (IRC § 121 is "bumped" by the new Act).

(5) Same facts as (1); except $750,000 of gain (house sells for $850,000).

Under facts of (1), (old law) *none* of gain would be recognized, due to reinvestment in new principal residence of a cost equal to or greater than the selling price of old house.

Under facts of (2), (old law) $625,000 of gain ($750,000 - $125,000) would be recognized due to the fact that there was no reinvestment.

Under new law $250,000 of gain would be recognized ($750,000 - $500,000) regardless of whether the proceeds are reinvested.

7.   One-Time Exclusion of Gain.

IRC § 121 is bumped by the approved legislation under the Tax Relief Act of 1997 effective for transactions on, or after May 7, 1997:

IRC § 121 One time exclusion of gain from a sale of principal residence by an individual who has attained the age of 55

IRC § 121(a) If the taxpayer has reached the age of 55 before the sale or exchange and the property has been used as the taxpayer's primary residence during three out of the five previous years then GI does not include gain from the sale or exchange.

IRC § 121(b) The amount of gain can not exceed $125,000 ($62,500 if not joint return).
*   This election can only be used once
*   If similar election made before July 26, 1978 then such election is not taken into account.

8.   Involuntary conversions: IRC § 1033

Involuntary conversions occur when the taxpayer's property is condemned and she receives an eminent domain award or if it is destroyed or stolen and she receives an insurance payment.
The code allows the taxpayer not to recognize such gain since it is unwanted. The purpose is to encourage productive activity and prevent compounding the injury.

IRC § 1033(a) If property as a result of destruction, seizure, requisition, condemnation is compulsorily, or involuntarily converted into:

IRC § 1033(a)(1) similar property no gain shall be recognized

IRC § 1033(a)(2) money or property not similar or related in service or use to the property destroyed, seized, requisitioned, condemned, etc., the gain shall be recognized unless:

IRC § 1033(a)(2)(A) The taxpayer purchases other property and the amount received for the conversion exceeds the cost of the replacement property:
* The property purchased must be of a similar or of related use or in a corporation owning such property
* The property must be purchased after the conversion.

IRC § 1033(a)(2)(B) Election to purchase new property must be made within 2 years of the close of the taxable year of the condemnation or a later date chosen by the secretary of state.

IRC § 1033(b)(1) Basis of the new property: Basis of the property converted decreased by any loss or increased by any gain.

IRC § 1033(g) Condemnation of real property held for productive use in trade or business for investment. If real property which is held for productive use in trade or business or investment, is condemned, property of like kind to be held for the same use shall be treated as similar property.

Gain = cash taken out
Only taxed to the extent cash is received.

Note:
* This section, unlike the other nonrecognition sections is elective and not mandatory
* The similar or related services tests is much stricter than the like kind test of § 1031.
* A fixture in a store does not equal a drill press and a drill press used by the taxpayer does not equal one that he rents out.
* However, if one is a lessor in both the new and the old property, that is similar even if the tenants are different.
* No gain is recognized if the proceeds are reinvested in like kind property, whether or not the property is similar or related in service

or use. Therefore, one can use the test of IRC § 1031. Additionally two years are allowed for the replacement of the property.

9.   Certain exchanges of insurance policies: IRC § 1035.
No gain or loss is recognized for swapping insurance contracts as long as it is a swap and no boot is paid.

VII. CAPITAL GAINS AND LOSSES

A. MAXIMUM TAX RATE ON NET CAPITAL GAIN

Prior to the 1997 Act, the maximum rate of tax that could be imposed in the realized "net capital gain" (i.e., the excess of long-term capital gain over net short-term capital loss) of an individual taxpayer was 28%.

Under "The Act of 1997," the maximum rate on net capital gain is reduced to 20% (10% percent for taxpayers who are in the 15% "ordinary income bracket) and 25% for certain depreciable real property.

The rate cut is implemented in a 2 step process:
  i.   In qualifying transactions on or after July 29, 1997 (see(2)), the maximum rate on net capital gain is 20%.

  ii.   Qualifying transactions from May 7, 1997 through July 29, 1997 will also qualify for the reduction in capital gain rates, even if the asset were held for less than 18 months, provided it was held at least 12 months and a day.

Note: Under "The Act of 1997" the holding period for long-term capital gain, an essential ingredient of "net capital gain" (IRC § 1222) is raised from more than 12 months to more than 18 months for post July 29, 1997 transactions.

Notice: of new tax developments as of July 10, 1998: Proposed changes effective upon the President signing into law. The Capital gains tax change would be effective retroactive for all sales as of January 1, 1998.

Change affects the homeowner.
If a home owner sells a home owned for less than two years the homeowner will be allowed partial relief based on a fraction rather than the owners actual profit.
For example:
If a single taxpayer homeowner makes $125,000 profit by selling his/her home owned for less than one year; that taxpayer would be allowed to exclude the entire $125,000 profit (gain), not just half the profit.
The hidden trap: Could mean higher taxes for homeowners who have *huge* short-term profits.

Change affects the investor with regard to the reduction of the asset holding period from 18 months to 12 months for assets (stocks) to qualify for the reduced 20% capital gains tax rate for sales of assets effective retroactive January 1, 1998.
Under the proposed law only gains on investments (stocks) held for less than the 12 months holding period will be taxed as ordinary income.

---

    1.   Generally

"Capital gain" is gain derived from the sale or exchange of a capital asset. Capital assets broadly include "property" of the taxpayer, typically investment property, in contrast to ordinary income from salaries, interests, dividends, profits, etc. Capital gain has historically been treated more favorably than ordinary income, but capital loss has generally been treated less favorably.

Taxpayer prefers capital gains and ordinary losses,
IRS wants ordinary gains and capital losses.

IRC § 1(h) Establishes the maximum tax rates applicable to individuals, and IRC § 1222 defines net capital gains/losses. To be eligible for favorable treatment, taxpayer must have a *net capital gain* -- i.e., an excess of net long-term gain over the net short-term capital loss (IRC § 1222(1)).

2. Capital Gain Or Ordinary Income

   a. **Capital Assets**

   To have capital gain or capital loss, there must be a *sale or exchange* of a *capital asset*. Without a capital asset, there can be neither a capital gain nor a capital loss. IRC § 1222.

   A capital asset is generally *all* the property held by the taxpayer, except:
   - i. property held for sale in the ordinary course of the taxpayer's business or inventory
   - ii. property used in the trade or business which is depreciable, or
   - iii. real property used in the trade or business (but see IRC § 1231),
   - iv. a "copyright", a literary, musical or artistic composition, a letter or memorandum, or similar property, held by the taxpayer who created it or for whom it was created, or whose basis is determined by reference to that of the creator. IRC § 1221(a)(1) - (5)

   b. **Leasehold Interests**
   * A lease = a property interest
   * Landlord's transaction with the tenant = ordinary since landlord retains an interest in the property
   * However, if the landlord pays the lessee for a cancellation or change in lease terms, then this is a capital gain for the tenant since tenant is selling his property right (See IRC § 1241)
   * Tenant selling his interest in a leasehold to a third party is a capital gain/loss since he retains no interest in the property
   * Compensation for the right to use property = ordinary income since no property interest is transferred.
   * Payment for a temporary taking by the government does not equal a capital gain.

   Hort v. Comm'r, 313 U.S.. 28 (1941)
   Hort paid the landlord to get out of the lease.
   Held: That this was ordinary income to landlord since it was merely a substitute for rent under IRC § 61. There was no sale or exchange of property.

McAllister v. Comm'r, 157 F. 2d. 235 (2d Cir. 1946) *cert. den'd.*, 330 U.S. 826 (1947).

A father leaves a trust in a will, the income of which is to be paid to his daughter-in-law for life with the remainder to his son. Life tenant had debts so she surrendered her interest for $55,000. This was substantially less than the interest was worth.

Held: This was a sale of interest in property, not an assignment of income. Therefore there should be capital not ordinary treatment.

Thus, a life estate may be "property" under IRC § 1221

Today: Under IRC § 1001(e) if a remainderman does not sell when the life tenant does, the Life Estate basis = 0. Thus, *McAllister* would show only a capital gain, not a loss.

Rule: The transfer of a portion of oil payments is a transfer of future income and not a property right. Therefore, transfer is ordinary income. (*Comm'r. v. PG Lake* 356 U.S. 260 (1958)

Miller v. Comm'r, 299 F. 2d 706 (2d Cir.) *cert. den'd.*, 370 U.S. 923 (1962) (Personal Rights are not the same as Property Rights)

Glen Miller's widow sold the rights to make a motion picture of her husband's life.

Held: This is a personal right which is not property. Therefore the sale is an ordinary gain, not a capital gain.

Rule: Not everything sold is property, for example, the right to vote, sue, experience life, privacy.

3. Losses on worthless securities: **IRC § 165(g)**

Any security that is a capital asset that becomes worthless shall be treated as a loss from the sale or exchange of property on the last day of the taxable year in which the security becomes worthless.

Note: Securities in affiliated corporations which are domestic corporations are not treated as capital assets. IRC § 165(g)(3). A corporation is "affiliated" when the taxpayer owns 80% of the stock of the corporation and more than 90% of all its income is from royalties, rents, dividends, interest, etc. IRC § 165(g)(3)(A)(B).

4. Determination of amount of gain or loss realized and recognized: **IRC § 1001**

IRC § 1001(c) recognition of gain or loss

Provides that the entire amount of the gain or loss realized upon the sale or exchange of property shall be recognized.

Note: To have current tax consequences, the gain or loss must be both *realized and recognized.*

* Non-recognition merely defers the gain or loss because the taxpayer takes the basis of the transferred property.

5. Four exceptions to this rule:
   a. Like Kind Exchange IRC § 1031
   b. Rollover House IRC § 1034
   c. One time exclusion IRC § 121
   d. Involuntary Conversion IRC § 1033

B. CAPITAL GAINS AND LOSSES

Maximum capital gains tax rate = 20% (for qualified transactions on or after May 7, 1997)

Caution: The maximum capital gains tax rate applies only where a taxpayer has a "net capital gain" for any taxable year. Net capital gain requires long-term, rather than short-term, gains. See IRC § 1222(11)

1. Short-term/Long-term Capital Gains and Losses: **IRC § 1222**

To have favorable tax treatment from capital transactions, it is necessary for a taxpayer to have a *net capital gain. A net capital gain*, as defined in IRC § 1222(11), involves a matching of the taxpayer's realized and recognized gains and losses - both long-term and short-term - from the *sale or exchange* of capital assets during the taxable year. *Capital loss carryforwards* or simply as *carryforward losses*, may also be considered. If the overall result of this matching process is that the taxpayer's net long-term gains (long-term gain *minus* long-term loss = net long-term gain/loss) exceed his net short-term losses (short-term gain, i.e., the *net long-term gain*, qualifies for the maximum tax rate of 28% (20% for **transactions entered into on or after May 7, 1997**) under IRC § 1(h).

Example 1:
During the current taxable year, Barnwell, an individual, has $12,000 of gains from the sale of stock he held for many years. He has no other capital asset transactions during the taxable year. Barnwell has a *net capital gain* for the taxable year of $12,000.
Example 2:

Example 2:
Same facts as in Example (1), except that Barnwell has only held the stock for 7 months. It has a $12,000 short-term capital gain which is taxable at his ordinary income rate.

Example 3:
The facts are the same as in example (1), except that Barnwell also realized and recognized $4,000 in losses from assets held for less than a year. For the current year, he has a *net capital gain* of $8,000.

Example 4:
The facts are the same as in example (1) except that Barnwell also realized and recognized losses. Barnwell has a net loss of $4,000 for the taxable year, which is not fully deductible due to the limitation in IRC § 1211(b). The loss is a *net long-term loss*, if the loss assets were held for more than a year and a *net short-term loss*, if held for a year or less. The part of Barnwell's loss that is not currently deductible may be carried forward indefinitely, subtract to characterization limitation under IRC § 1212 discussed *infra*.

Note: "The 1997 Act"
The 12 month and 1 day holding period generally applicable under prior law is preserved for transactions entered into on or after May 7, 1997 through July 28, 1997; thereafter, a capital asset must be held for 18 months to be classified as long-term. Additional changes, pertaining to capital transactions in the "1997 Act" that promise to have significant impact are :

    a.   in 2001, the maximum rate is scheduled to decline further to 18% for capital assets acquired after 2000 and held for more than five years;

    b.   individuals can "roll over" the gain on small business stock" in IRC § 1202, provided the stock has been held for more than 6 months and the proceeds are reinvested within 60 days in qualifying stock; and

    c.   the gain on certain real property transactions will be taxed at 25% tax rate, to the extent not already "recaptured."

2. Limitation on capital losses: IRC § 1211

*   Corporations can only deduct losses from sale or exchange of capital assets to the extent of capital gains (IRC § 1211(a).

*   Excess losses may be carried *back* up to 3 years and *forward* up to 5 years (IRC § 1212(a)).

*   Other noncorporate taxpayers can deduct capital losses from the sale or exchange of capital assets to the extent of the capital gains plus the lower of $3,000 or the excess of such losses over gains (IRC § 1211(b)(1) and (2)

*   Excess losses of a noncorporate taxpayer may be carried *forward* indefinitely, subject to characterization rules in IRC § 1212(b) until used up.

3. Capital loss carrybacks and carry-overs: IRC § 1212
In general, capital losses are fully deductible, provided they do not exceed the taxpayer's capital gains. IRC § 1211(a) In addition to offsetting capital gains, taxpayers who are not corporations may deduct up to $3,000 of *excess* capital losses against ordinary income. IRC § 1211(b) The balance, if any, may be carried forward indefinitely as long-term or short-term capital loss, as the case may be, until used up. IRC § 1212(b)

Corporate taxpayers, in contrast, are **ineligible to deduct** *excess* **capital** losses, but may carry the excess back as a short-term capital loss for up to 3 years and then forward for up to 5 years. IRC § 1212(a)(1)

Noncorporate taxpayers:
i.   may carry forward as a *net short-term capital loss* to succeeding taxable years the *excess* of the taxpayer's *net short-term capital loss* over the taxpayer's *net long-term capital gain* (IRC § 1212(b)(1)(A)); and
ii. may carryforward as a *net long-term capital loss* the *excess* of the taxpayer's *net long-term capital losses* over the taxpayer's *net short-term capital gains*. IRC § 1212(b)(1)(B)

Example for the application of IRC § 1212:
An individual taxpayer has $5,000 of capital gains and $13,000 of capital losses. Broken down into long-term and short-term gains and losses, he has $4,000 of long-term gains and $10,000 of long-term

losses. He also has $1,000 in short-term gains and short-term losses of $3,000.

Of these facts, the taxpayer reports total gains of $5,000 and deducts total losses of $5,000. That is, he matches gains and losses, as prescribed by IRC § 1211(b). He also deducts an additional $3,000 of excess losses. Thus, the taxpayer reports $5,000 of capital gains and deducts $8,000 in capital losses. What is left to be carried forward? The task of IRC § 1212 is to:

    i.   determine the amount of unused capital loss available to be carried forward.

    ii. To characterize the loss as short-term or long-term as the case might be.

Analysis:

IRC § 1212(b)(1) provides that the excess of net short-term capital loss over the net long-term capital gain for the taxable year is to be carried forward as a short-term capital loss in succeeding taxable years. In addition, the excess of net long-term capital loss over net short-term capital gain is to be carried forward as a long-term capital loss in succeeding years.

In making these calculations, however, IRC § 1212(b)(2) provides that the $3,000 of additional loss allowed under IRC § 1211(b)(1) or (2) is to be treated as a short-term capital loss.

Thus, for purposes of determining the taxpayer's carryforward losses, he has no net short-term capital losses when the adjustment required by IRC § 1212(b)(2) is made (actual short-term capital gains $1,000 + $3,000 of deemed short-term capital gain under IRC § 1212(b)(2) = $3,000 *minus* $3,000 short-term capital loss = 0 net short-term capital/gain/loss carryforward)

On the long-term side, the taxpayer's long-term capital loss carryforward is determined by the excess of his net long-term losses over his net short-term capital gains (IRC § 1212(b)(1)(B). Here, IRC § 1212(b)(2)(A) provides that the additional loss deductible under IRC § 1211(b)(1) or (2) is to be treated as a ***short-term*** capital gain in the taxable year.

Plugging this into the computation required by IRC § 1212(b)(1)(B), the taxpayer has a $5,000 net long-term capital loss carryforward. This carryforward is determined by comparing $6,000 of net long-term capital loss to his net short-term gain of $1,000 [short-term gain of $1,000 (actual) and $3,000 (constructed by statute from the additional loss allowable under IRC § 1211(b)(1) or (2)) less actual short-term capital loss of $3,000 = $1,000 net short-term gain].

The taxpayer thus begins his next taxable year with $5,000 of capital loss carryforward, properly characterized as a net long-term capital loss of $5,000, which he will absorb against a like amount of capital gain in that next taxable year.

The net effect of treating the additional loss deduction committed IRC § 1211(b)(1) or (2) is to require the taxpayer to charge short-term losses first to the extent of such losses and then long-term losses, if any.

4.   50% Exclusion for gains on small business stock: **IRC § 1202**.

*   For taxpayers other than corporations, GI does not include 50% of gains from the sale of small business stock issued after 1993 and held for more than 5 years. (IRC § 1202(a))

*   Gain subject to the 50 % exclusion cannot exceed the greater of $10,000,000 or ten times the adjusted basis of the stock being sold. (IRC § 1202(b)).

*   Qualified Small Business Stock = issued after Aug. 1993, Taxpayer = original purchaser, and the corporation must conduct an active business and have assets after stock issued not exceeding $50 million (not including farms, banks, insurance, leasing investing etc., motel hotel, restaurant, etc., IRC § 1202(d)).

The 1997 Act significantly expands the impact of § 1202 with   IRC § 1045.

5.   Summary of the new: IRC § 1045.

Permits the deferral of gain recognition attributable to the sale of qualified small business stock held for more than 6 months, provided that within 60 days of the date of sale, the proceeds of the sale are used to purchase other qualified small business stock.

VIII. ASSIGNMENT OF INCOME

A. INTRODUCTION

Once it has been determined that a particular item is "income" within the general scope of IRC § 61 or a more specific Code provision, the *identity* of the taxpayer becomes critical. The potential significance of this issue can be illustrated with the following examples:

Example 1:
During 1997, A and B, who are married taxpayers who ordinarily file a joint income tax return, had *Taxable Income* in excess of $250,000. In December 1997, A received a check for $1,000, which represented a dividend paid by a closely held corporation in which she owned 10 shares of stock.

Since A and B are "cash method," "calendar year" taxpayers, i.e., they account for items of income when they are actually or constructively received, and expenses when actually paid (Reg § 1.1446-1(i)(ii)(iii)), the dividend is reportable by A and B on their tax return for the period January 1 through December 31, 1997, and will generate $396 in additional taxes (due to the fact that A and B are in the 39.6% marginal tax bracket). A later gives $604 [$1000 **dividend** *less* **taxes**] to her child, C, in a transaction excluded from C's income due to IRC § 102. C receives, and keeps $604.

Example 2:
The facts are the same as in Example 1, except that A gave C the 10 shares of stock sometime prior to 1997. When the dividend is paid in 1997, it is properly taxed to C. C had no other income for 1997. C receives, and keeps $1,000.
What is necessary to bring about the result in Example (2)? The answers to this question depend on principles, which are generally grouped under the heading of this chapter, "Assignment of Income," and have been developed largely from decided cases and rulings. In this area, there are relatively few pertinent statutory provisions. However, when such provisions exist, they are enormously important.

Note:
* Tax returns for individual taxpayers are due by April 15th of the year following the close of the individual taxpayer's calendar year. When taxpayer reports on the basis of a fiscal year, or on a day other than April 15th, the due date for the return is "the 15th day of the fourth month following the close of the taxpayer's fiscal year."
* Tax brackets are "indexed" i.e., adjusted for changes in the consumer price index (CPI) on an annual basis.

B. INCOME DERIVED FROM PERSONAL SERVICES: SPLITTING OF INCOME

General Rule: Income is taxed to the person or persons who have dominion and control over the source of the income. With regard to compensation for personal services, the person who renders the services has ultimate control over the source of the income (i.e., the services).

Lucas v. Earl, 281 U.S. 111 (1930). Income was taxed to husband (H) who received salary and attorney's fees as compensation for his services, even though wife (W) had the contract rights, which Court *presumed* to be enforceable under local California law. Notwithstanding the fact that W became an owner of one-half the salary and fees:

> ". . . on the very first instant they were received . . .
> [the resolution of tax issues is not dependent on such]
> attenuated subtleties . . . [but rather] on the import
> and reasonable construction of the taxing act. There
> is no doubt that the statute could tax salaries to those
> who earned them and provide that the tax could not be
> escaped by anticipatory arrangements . . . however
> skillfully devised to prevent the salary when paid
> from vesting even for a second in the man who earned
> it . . . ."

Finally, the decision concludes with the well known metaphor of the "fruit" (income) and the "tree" (source). That is, income is not to be attributed to a "different tree [than] that on which [it] grew."

Result: Wife gets one-half the income, but Husband gets 100% of tax liability.

Note:
Specific result in *Lucas v. Earl* is not as significant today, at least for taxpayers who are married. "Split" of income can now be achieved by merely filing a joint income tax return (IRC § 1(a)).

* Result in *Lucas v. Earl* s should be contrasted with *Giannini v. Comm'r.*, 129 F.2d 638 (9th Cir. 1942) (taxpayer entitled to refuse to accept services-based income, *provided* he does not direct its disposition).

* Joint return IRC § 6013 permits married taxpayers to file a joint return. In effect, this permits each taxpayer to be taxed on all of the income from the marriage regardless of who earns it. This generally reduces the overall tax liability since each is taxed in a lower bracket. See IRC § 1(a).

* Where services are performed by an agent for a disclosed principal, the income is taxed to the principal who is entitled to it, rather than the agent who is not. *See* Rev. Rul. 74-581, 1974-2 C.B. 25 (fees paid to law school on account of services rendered by member of law school's clinical faculty were not taxed to faculty member who was otherwise compensated for his services and had previously agreed to turn over all such fees to the law school); see Rev. Rul. 69-274, 1969-1 C.B. 36

C. Income Derived From Property

In contrast to income attributable to the rendition of personal services, income derived from property - typically, rents, royalties, interest and dividends - may be assigned under appropriate circumstances.

The most important factor in achieving the desired "split" - and consequent tax savings - is to establish that there was a "shift" in dominion and control over the property from the Assignor to the Assignee.

* See *Helvering v. Horst*, 311 U.S. 112 (1940) (owner of interest-bearing bonds taxed on the interest even though interest coupons were physically detached from bonds and given to owner's son. Owner retained dominion and control over source of the interest income - the bonds - and, consequently was taxable on it.

* "Ordinarily . . . the taxpayer who acquires the right to receive income is taxed when he receives it, regardless of the time when his right to receive payment accrues . . . ."

Nonetheless, income may be realized when the taxpayer has made use or disposition of his power to receive or control the income as to produce in its place other satisfactions which are of economic worth. Income may therefore be "realized" when he who owns or controls the source of the income, also controls the disposition of that which he could have received himself and diverts payment from himself to others as the means of procuring the satisfaction of his wants. The taxpayer has equally enjoyed the fruits of his labor or investment . . .whenever he collects and uses the income to procure those satisfactions, or whether he disposes of his right to collect it as the means of procuring them [citations omitted]."

Real Property In a Community Property State:

Poe v. Seaborn, 282 U.S. 101 (1930)
Income diverted by operation of law. Real estate property was in the husband's name alone, but since the property was in a community property state the property was owned by both of them. Thus, unlike *Earl*, the law made the income divided into two rather than a private contract
Held: That they could each file separate returns. Where property is owned by each spouse by virtue of a community property statute, as opposed to a private agreement, the husband and wife are each taxed separately on his or her half regardless of who earns the income.

D. PERSONAL SERVICES OR PROPERTY?

It is not always easy to tell whether income is derived from services or property. Questions typically arise when the services have been performed, but payment has not yet occurred. If the cash method service provider assigns his/her *right to be paid* to another taxpayer, is this an assignment of a property right or merely compensation for services? The cases are unfortunately muddled.

Compare, for example:

Helvering v. Eubank, 311 U.S. 122 (1940)
Commissions earned by insurance agent attributable to renewal policies were treated as labor-based income. Therefore, commissions were taxable to the agent, even though eventually assigned. The assignor (insurance agent) was taxed as and when payments for such services were ultimately paid out to assignee.

Heim v. Fitzpatrick, 262 F. 2d 887 (2d Cir. 1959).
A gift of a patent from assignor's invention carried out income attributable to the patent to the assignee. The patent was "property" rather than mere compensation for the act of invention.

Blair v. Comm'r, 300 U.S. 5 (1937)
Taxpayer's sole interest in a trust was that of an income beneficiary for life. He assigned a "slice" of his right to receive income for the balance of his life.
Held: Taxpayer's assignment of right to receive income up to a specific dollar amount constituted a transfer of "property" sufficient to cause income tax consequences associated with the income derived from the property held in trust to be taxed to the assignee. Taxpayer had given up a slice of all that he had to surrender.

Contra, however:
0Harrison v. Schaffner, 312 U.S. 579 (1941) (taxpayer's assignment of specific dollar amounts of income on an annual basis merely shifted "income" rather than "property" consequently, beneficiaries - assignor - remained taxable on the income even though paid to the assignee)

But, the Tax Court's decision in *Hundley v. Comm'r.*, 48 TC 339 (1967), suggests a different approach that may achieve essentially the same result, though not on purely Assignment of Income principles. Taxpayer permitted to treat portion of bonus paid to him on signing professional baseball contract as *deductible* business expense, even though it was his first professional contract and bonus was paid to his father. Tax Court found that the obligation to pay was genuine and that son was "carrying on" a trade or business, since obligation to pay did not arise until he became a professional ballplayer.

Contra, however:
Allen v. Comm'r, 50 TC 466 (1968) (approach similar to *Hundley* failed where coaching fee was paid to player's mother whom the court found knew very little about baseball)

E. PROPERTY HELD IN TRUST

In general. When a taxpayer creates a trust and funds it with income-producing property, the issue of who is responsible for the tax becomes somewhat more complicated due to the rules applicable to trusts. *However, these rules do not even come into play unless the **basic** assignment of income principles have been satisfied.*

Example 1:
If Parent assigns 50% of his salary to his children, he remains liable for 100% of the tax liability, regardless of whether the salary is paid to the children outright or is held by a trust for their benefit.

Example 2:
Facts are the same as Example (1), except that Parent assigns an undivided one-half interest in income-producing bonds he owns to his children. Since the source of the income is the bonds, the income is *assignable.* The question of liability for tax on interest produced by the bonds will depend on the terms of the trust that holds the bonds. *See* Taxation of Trusts, *infra.*

F. TAXATION OF TRUSTS

1. In General.
*   Tax is imposed by Section 1(e).
*   Tax is imposed on **taxable income (TI)** of any trust or estate.
*   Rates are *high* (39.6% rate applies when TI exceeds $7,500).
*   Trusts are taxed "in the manner of an individual" (IRC § 641 (b).
*   Where the taxpayer transfers property to a trust in which the benefits are split between one or more charitable entities "private" i.e., non charitable interests, special restrictions apply. Failure to comply with these restrictions even in a relatively minor technical way may mean complete loss of this charitable contribution. The "1997 Act" tightens these restrictions.
*   If trust is "simple," i.e., if trustee must distribute all trust income annually (IRC §§ 651, 652), the trust is a "conduit" or "flow-through" entity. Trust files a tax return which claims a "distribution deduction" (IRC § 651) for trust income required to be distributed currently (whether or not distributed). The beneficiary reports amount of trust income required to be distributed currently (IRC § 652).

Example:
Trust holds income-producing property which produces
$10,000 of income in a particular taxable year. If the terms of the trust
require that all income is to be distributed currently, income is
nevertheless, reportable by trust which deducts the entire $10,000;

Result:
Trust has no tax liability for the year. Income "flows out"
to beneficiary and is taxed to him/her.

* If the trust is "complex" -- i.e., if terms of a trust permit
  accumulation of income (all trust income is *not* required to be
  distributed currently and beneficiary reports sum of:
  a. income required to be distributed currently; and
  b. any other income which is distributable under the terms of the
      trust The trust, in turn, takes a deduction for:
      i.   all income required to be distributed currently, and
      ii. income permitted to be distributed under the terms of the
           trust (IRC § 661, 662).

Example:
Assume the same facts as in the previous example, except
that the terms of the trust permit the trustee "in his sole and absolute
discretion," to distribute such amounts of trust income or principal as
the trustee may determine. If the trust's income in a particular taxable
year is $10,000, and the trustee distributes $5,000 to the beneficiary,
the trust reports gross income of $10,000 *less* a $5,000 distribution
deduction (IRC § 661); and the beneficiary reports $5,000, the amount
of trust income, properly distributable to him/her (IRC § 662).

2. Tax imposed: IRC § 641

For the purpose of the tax imposed by IRC § 1(e), IRC § 641 provides
that the taxable income of the trust or an estate is to be computed "in
the manner of an individual," with specified adjustments. IRC §
641(c) specifically provides that for purposes of computing the taxable
income of a trust, any "included gain" within IRC § 644 is not to be
taken into account.

3. Distributable net income (DNI) **IRC § 643**

Taxable income of the trust: (maximum amount that may be included in the beneficiaries' income and deducted as a distribution by the trust).

Distributable Net Income (DNI) is a key concept in the taxation of trusts. In substance, DNI is the effective limitation on the amount of a trust's taxable income that may be included in the income of the beneficiary in any particular year. Moreover, DNI limits the amount of distribution deduction that may be claimed by the trust. Thus, if the amount currently distributable to a beneficiary exceeds the trust's DNI, the distribution deduction is limited to the amount of DNI, not the amount required to be distributed currently.

4. Special rule for gain on property transferred to trust at less than fair market value: **IRC § 644**.

Section 644 provides, in general, that when a Grantor transfers appreciated property to a trust and the trust sells it within two years thereafter, that portion of the appreciation which existed on the date of the transfer to the trust is to be taxed as though sold by the grantor. Thus, it is not taken into account for purposes of determining the taxable income of the trust, because it has already been accounted for.

5. Simple trust: **IRC § 651**.

If all income of the trust is required to be currently distributed to the beneficiary and no corpus distributions are made and no deductions for charity are made, then the trust can deduct the payment of income made.

6. Inclusion of amounts in gross income of beneficiaries of trusts distributing current income only: **IRC § 652**.

The amount of income required to be distributed currently under IRC § 651 is included in the GI of the beneficiary whether distributed or not. The excess over DNI is prorated among beneficiaries.
* The trust is taxed on capital gains allocated to corpus.
* The character of the income in the hands of the trustee is the same when in the hands of the beneficiary (i.e., capital gain, tax exempt interest).

7. Deduction for estates and trusts accumulating income or
    distributing corpus: **IRC § 661.**

Where trustee is permitted to accumulate income rather than distribute
it, the trust gets a deduction only and is not taxed for what it
distributes.

8. Inclusion of amounts in gross income of beneficiaries of estates
    and trusts: **IRC § 662.**

Beneficiary (i) includes in GI the sum of what the trustee is required to
distribute currently; and (ii) any amounts that are distributed to the
beneficiary. Required distributions below DNI are included in the GI of
the beneficiaries.

* Beneficiary is either taxed on the lesser of (i) DNI or (ii) GI from
   distributions.

9. Throwback Rules.

If the trust accumulates income, then it is taxed on that income. If the
trust then distributes the income the following year as corpus, the
beneficiary is taxed on it again. However the beneficiaries' tax is
reduced by the tax that the trust paid.

Note:
The "1997 Act" *takes out* the Throwback Rules effective August 5,
1997

10. Charitable Remainder Trust.

Charitable Remainder Trust is a form of trust typically used to
avoid capital gains when making gifts to charity.

The "Tax Relief Act of 1997" sets a maximum percentage for the
charity's share of the trust. This can be expected to reduce the number
of Charitable Remainder Trusts.

11. Grantor Trusts.

A grantor with effective dominion and control over a trust is taxed on
income attributable to the trust or the portion of the trust over which

she has control. For example, if a grantor can direct the enjoyment of current income, she is taxed on the income. In contrast, if the grantor can allocate gains from any sales from property held by the trust, the grantor is treated as the "owner" of the capital gain and taxed accordingly.

The concept of "ownership" of a trust grew out of case law. *See, e.g.,* Helvering v Clifford, 309 US 331 (1940) (husband taxed on income of trust established by him for the benefit of his wife. Court found that grantor had complete dominion and control over the trust, notwithstanding the apparent cessation of his interest in the property used to fund the trust). However, since 1954, the issue of who is to be treated as "owner" of the trust and or principal is exclusively statutory (see IRC §§ 671 through 678).

In general, the grantor is treated as the owner of any "portion" of a trust in which the grantor, or a "non-adverse party" or both have an interest in, or power over, the enjoyment of that portion of the trust. For example, if the grantor creates a trust and retains the power to revoke it with or without the consent of a person who has no interest in the trust, the grantor is treated as the owner of the trust regardless of whether the grantor ever exercises the power. It is immaterial that trust income is actually paid to the beneficiaries or not. This is due to the grantor's ability to change the entire trust scenario at any time. In contrast, if the grantor required the consent of the beneficiaries, i.e., parties who are "adverse", the grantors powers would be deemed to be negated.

12. Trust income, deductions, and credits attributable to grantor trusts and others as substantial owners: **IRC § 671.**

If the grantor "owns" a trust, or a "portion" of a trust, then the income from that "portion" of a trust is taxable to him, as though the trust did not exist. For this purpose "ownership" means that the grantor, or a non-adverse party, or both, can control beneficial enjoyment or has the right to enjoy it himself.

G. DEFINITIONS AND RULES: IRC § 672.

1. Adverse Person.

An "adverse" party is a person with a substantial beneficial interest in the trust which will be adversely affected if the grantor's power is exercised.

Example 1:
The grantor retains the right to divert trust income from the income beneficiary of a trust. The grantor is deemed to "own" the income from the trust, regardless of whether he ever exercises the power.

Example 2:
The facts are the same as in the previous example except that in order to divert trust income, the grantor requires the consent of the income beneficiary. The income beneficiary is an adverse party. The requirement that he consent negates the grantor's power and the general rules applicable to revocating trust income tax liability among the trust and the beneficiary apply. *See* IRC §§ 651, 652, 661 and 662, discussed above.

2. Reversionary interest (Clifford Doctrine): **IRC § 673.**

The grantor is taxed as the owner of any trust in which he has a reversionary interest greater than 5%

3. Power to control beneficial enjoyment: **IRC § 674.**

IRC § 674(b) Specifies limited exceptions to the general rule where that the grantor possesses the power to control beneficial enjoyment, the grantor is treated as the "owner" of the trust. The statute specifies that the following powers will not cause the grantor to be treated as owner: (i) power to supply income to support a beneficiary (except where the grantor's support obligation may be discharged); (ii) conditional exercise on the occurrence of an event; (iii) power that may be exercisable only by Will; (iv) power to allocate among various charities; (v) power to temporarily withhold income; (vi) power to allocate between corpus and income distribution; (vii) power to allocate limited by an ascertainable standard.

4.   Administrative Powers: IRC § 675.

Grantor can be treated as the owner if unusual powers can be exercised by the grantor, non-adverse party or both without the consent of an adverse party.
Example:
*   make deals for less than adequate consideration
*   loan from the trust without adequate interest or security. Without authorization by an independent trustee
*   borrowing from the trust fund without repaying in full by the beginning of the year
*   power to vote stocks, substitute corpus, control investments

5.   Power to revoke: IRC § 676

Grantor is the owner of a trust, if he or a non-adverse party retains the power to revoke the trust, unless it is conditioned on an event that is sufficiently defined so that, if it were a reversionary interest in the grantor, it would be worth 5% or less of the value of the portion of the trust over which the grantor can exercise his power. See IRC § 673(a).

6.   Income for benefit of grantor: IRC § 677.

Where the grantor is the direct or indirect beneficiary of a trust, the grantor is treated as the owner of the trust income. Where the trust income may be used to discharge a support obligation of the grantor, IRC § 677(b) provides that the mere existence of this possibility does not cause the grantor to be taxed currently, but only as and when the income is so used.

7.   Person other than the grantor treated as substantial owner:
      IRC § 678.

If a party other than the grantor has the power to vest the corpus or income in his name, or has some of the powers which make a grantor the owner of the trust, such person shall be treated as the owner of the trust.
Exceptions.   This shall not apply:
*   if given the power to discharge an obligation of support, then only taxed to the extent that the power is used;
*   if the power is disclaimed, then the grantor is not taxed

However, if the grantor is the owner due to another section of the code, then the grantor will be taxed as the owner.

Brooke v. U.S. 468 F.2d 1155 (9th Cir. 1972)
Father makes a gift of property to his children and then leases the property back. the gift is unconditional and unrevocable. He has no individual control, all funds are exercised for the children's benefit. All dispositions require court approval
Held: That the children, donees, are taxed since they own the property.
    a.   full transfer, no retained power
    b.   no control retained by donor
    c.   money used for donee's benefit
    d.   trustee is independent

IX. BUSINESS ASSOCIATIONS

A. PARTNERSHIPS

Partnerships are not treated as separate entities for tax purposes. Each partner is individually liable for his/her share of income generated by the partnership (IRC § 701). Under IRC § 702, partnership income, deductions and credits are allocated among the partners based upon their "distributive share" (IRC § 704) of the partnership.

To be valid for tax purposes, a partnership must be formed for a valid business purpose. One must look at the intent and conduct of the parties, and whether there was a bona fide attempt to create a partnership. (*Comm'r. v. Culbertson*, 337 U.S. 733 (1949); IRC § 704(e)).

1. Partners, not partnership, is subject to tax: **IRC § 701.**

* Partnership is not treated as a separate entity.
* Partners are liable for income taxes "flowed-through" to them, regardless of whether the income is actually distributed.

2. Income and credits of partner: **IRC § 702.**

Each partner's income tax is determined by his distributive share of the partnership. Actual distribution of income is not required. Partnership income "flowed through" to a partner increases the partner's basis in his/her partnership interest. When income is actually distributed, basis is reduced accordingly (IRC § 705).

Partner's "flowed thru" income includes: Business gains and losses from capital assets, exchanges of property, charitable contributions, taxes, income, gain, loss, deduction, credits, etc.

3. Partnership computations: **IRC § 703.**

Partnership computations have limitations of what partners may deduct from income.

Computed the same as an individual except that certain items must be stated separately and certain deductions cannot be deducted from the partnership income; e.g., IRC § 151 personal exemptions, IRC § 164 taxes, IRC § 172 charitable deductions, IRC § 172 net operating loss, and IRC §§ 67, 162, 212 individual itemized deductions.

4.   Partner's distributive share: **IRC § 704.**

Determined by the partnership agreement or if not specified, determined
by each partner's interest in the partnership.

   a.   Family partnerships
   IRC § 704(e) Family partnerships - Person is a partner if a
   capital interest in a partnership is acquired by gift or by purchase.
   Requirement is used to distinguish shift of income to property and
   mere service-based income. *See* Chapter VIII: Assignment of
   Income. For example if a family member, such as a child, is given
   a partnership interest without contributing capital to the partnership,
   the income attributable to the partnership interest can be,
   nonetheless, shifted unless it is a service business, such as that
   conducted by a doctor or lawyer.

   Note:
   *   The underlying capital investment may be shifted, not the
       management interest
   *   If services are the material income-producing factor, then they
       can not be shifted
   *   Look at the intent of the parties and their conduct.

   Culbertson v. Comm'r., (337 U.S. 733 (1949)
   A taxpayer (TP) buys out his partner's interest and makes his
   children partners. TP attempts to split partnership income among
   his children and himself. Commissioner claimed TP was sole
   recipient of the income for tax purposes.
   Held: This was a partnership only if there were significant
   contributions of capital or services by the partners. The partners
   must also show good-faith with a business purpose for creating the
   partnership.

   *   Today IRC § 704(e) is used to determine if a partnership exists

   U.S. v. Basye, 410 U.S. 441 (1973)
   Partnership was paid in the form of a retirement fund, even though
   the income was not distributed.
   Held: That the income must be included in the GI of the partners
   for the year that it was paid, since income must be taxed to the
   person who earns it.

b. Pass-thru of items to shareholders: IRC § 1366.

IRC § 1366(e) In a family group, if an individual who is a shareholder in an S corporation makes a donation or renders service without receiving reasonable compensation, there will be adjustments in her share to reflect the capital or service contributions.

B. CORPORATIONS

1. Corporate Taxation

    a. Corporations are taxed on a "double" tax model:
        i. Corporation is treated as a separate entity with no deductions for dividends paid (IRC § 11).
        ii. Under IRC § 61 (a) (7), shareholders pay tax on dividends distributed to them.

    b. Tax imposed on corporations: IRC § 11.

    Historically, corporations have been taxed at lower marginal tax rates than individual taxpayers. This has led to a desire to accumulate earnings and profits at the corporate level, rather than distributing them as nondeductible dividends. *See* "penalty" tax on accumulated earning (IRC § 531) and the tax on personal holding company income (IRC § 541).

2. Limitation on use of cash method of accounting: IRC § 448.

IRC § 448(d)(2) Qualified personal service corporation means any corporation that in principle performs services in health, law, engineering, architecture, accounting, performing arts, or consulting, and whose stock is held primarily by the employees performing the services, retired employees, or estates of such employees.
* Is taxed not at the graduated rate, but at a flat 35%
* In general, a personal service corporation may not use the cash method of accounting and must use the calendar year as its taxable period (IRC §§ 444; 448; but see IRC § 448 (c)).

3.   Allocation of income and deductions among corporations:
     IRC § 482

If there is common control by a corporation of two or more businesses, the IRS can allocate income, deductions and credits between or among them to accurately and clearly reflect the income and to prevent tax evasion.

Fogelsong v. Comm'r., 621 F.2d 865 (7th Cir. 1980).
Taxpayer worked for two corporations as a salesman. He then formed his own corporation. TP's children owned a large portion of preferred stock and he caused the corporation to pay dividends to them. He took considerably less in income than the corporation made. All corporate formalities were followed.
Held: That this was permissible, neither IRC § 482 nor (Lucas v. Earl) were applicable since this was a functioning corporation which had contracts for the work.
*   Today we have a "Kiddie tax" whereby children under 14 are taxed at their parents' bracket. Thus, this type of benefit is no longer available.

Sargent v. Comm'r., 929 F.2d 1254 (8th Cir. 1991).
Hockey player gave his income to a personal service corporation which he formed. The money went from the hockey team to the corporation to the player.
He siphoned off money through a pension plan, accumulated in the corporation's lower bracket.
Held: Income was taxed to the player, who was the provider of the services. The Appeals Court reversed under a two prong test.
> i.   Service provider must be an employee of the corporation and with whom the corporation has a right to direct or control in a meaningful sense.
> ii. A contract must exist between the corporation and the receiver of the services.

Held also: That the corporation, not the team is in control of the player. To successfully shift income to a corporation, it is necessary to observe all corporate formalities and the corporation must be formed for a valid business purpose. Nonetheless, the flat rate applicable to personal service corporations (IRC §11(b)(2)) tends to mitigate much of the benefits sought.

Johnson v. Comm'r., 78 T.C. 882 (1982).
Similar to *Sargent*, however player contracted with corporation and
expected his team to pay the corporation for his services. He was paid
the salary and then assigned it to the personal service corporation.
Held: That this is like *Lucas v. Earl* . The player, not his wholly
owned corporation, is taxable on compensation income derived from the
player's services. and the taxpayer, each partner is individually liable for
his/her share of income generated by the partnership (IRC § 701). Under
IRC
§ 702, partnership income, deductions and credits are allocated among the
partners based upon their "distributive share" (IRC § 704) of the
partnership.

4.   Exemption from tax on corporations: **IRC § 501.**

Corporations are tax-exempt if they used for religious, charitable,
scientific, literary, or educational purposes or to foster amateur sports
(providing facilities or equipment) or prevention of cruelty to children or
animals (Similar to IRC § 170).
*   Not applicable if a club discriminates on the basis of religion, race
      or color

Bob Jones v. U.S., 461 U.S. 574 (1983).
University banned interracial dating for religious reasons.
Held: Denied deduction, no exempt status for institutions that fall
under IRC § 501(c)(3) if they pursue policies contrary to public policy.

X. METHODS OF ACCOUNTING

In general, tax accounting is a question of timing -- when income is received for tax purposes and when expenses are deductible.

The taxpayer wants to pay later and the IRS wants the money now.

A. IN GENERAL.

1. Taxable Year: **IRC § 441.**

Regardless of the taxpayer's method of accounting, income, deductions and credits are accounted for on the basis of the taxpayer's taxable year. In general, the taxable year is the taxpayer's "annual accounting period" (i.e., ". . . the annual period on the basis of which the taxpayer regularly computes his income in keeping his books.") The annual accounting period must be either a "calendar year . . . a period of twelve months ending on December 31," or a fiscal year ". . . a period of twelve months ending on the last day of any month other than December."

2. General rule for methods of accounting: **IRC § 446.**

* Taxable income is computed using a regularly employed method of accounting. IRC § 446(a);
* If there is no regularly employed method, or method does not *clearly reflect income,* the taxpayer can select method set out in IRC § 446(c).

A taxpayer engaged in more than one trade or business may use different methods of accounting for each trade or business, provided the method used clearly reflects income.

Once the taxpayer has adopted a method of accounting, the Service's approval is needed to change the accounting method used.

Apart from special situations, such as inventories, the most commonly used methods are the cash receipts and disbursements method and the accrual method.

Cash Method - Income is included in the year in which it is actually or constructively received. Expenses are deducted when actually or constructively paid (IRC § 5446(c)(1); Reg § 1.446-1(c)(3)(i))

Accrual Method - Income is recorded at the time earned even if not paid. Deduction is made when expense obligation is incurred not when actually paid (IRC § 5446(c)(2); Reg § 1.446-1(c)(1)(i)).

Any other method, or combination of methods, may be utilized, subject to the "clear reflection of income" limitation and the permission of the Service.

B. METHODS OF ACCOUNTING IN DETAIL

1. Cash Method.

   a. C Corporations May Not Use Cash Method.
   In general, C corporations, partnerships in which a C corporation is a partner, or tax shelters may *not* use the cash method of accounting. IRC § 448(a).

   Reg. § 1.446-1(c) (1) (i) provides that ". . . under the cash receipts and disbursements method in the computation of taxable income, all items which constitute gross income (whether in the form of cash, property, or services) are to be included for the **taxable year in which actually or constructively received.**" [emphasis added] Expenditures are to be deducted for the taxable year in which actually made.

   b. The Cash Method Illustrated
   The cash receipts and disbursements method is easily illustrated.

   Example 1:
   A receives $1000 in *cash* on December 28 of Year One. If the $1000 received represents salary to A, it is taxable to him as compensation income under IRC § 61(a) 1) in Year One, the year of receipt.

   Example 2:
   The result in the preceding example would not change even if A received a *check* for $1000 from his employer on December 28. The

receipt of a check is considered a "cash equivalent" and is treated like the receipt of cash. IRC § 83.

c.   Rules Under Cash Method.

Rules for inclusion/deduction under cash receipt and disbursements method of recording:

Economic Benefit Theory: Despite apparent restrictions on the use of the item received, under the cash receipts and disbursements method, the *receipt* of the item, rather than a practical ability to use it at the particular time received, is the crucial event. Thus, the cash or check received by the employer, A, as compensation in the year in which it is received. It is immaterial that it may have been received after the close of business so that it could not be readily used. However, if the item received, such as an option to buy stock, is subject to a **substantial risk of forfeiture,** the item will not be taxed until the substantial risk of forfeiture lapses. See IRC § 83.

Constructive Receipt: if a cash method taxpayer has an unqualified right to a sum of money and the power to obtain it, then he has constructively received it and it can be counted as current income even if he chooses not to receive it. However, there is no constructive receipt, if taxpayer's control of its receipt is subject to substantial limitations or restrictions.

Reg. § 1.451-2(a) provides that in the case of interest, dividends, or other earnings (whether or not credited) payable in respect of banks and other financial institutions, the requirement that the deposit or account and any earnings be withdrawn in multiples of even amounts or that the deposit or withdrawal be made subject to a forfeiture of interest to which the taxpayer would be entitled had he left the account on deposit until a later date, do not constitute "substantial restriction." Reg. §1.451-2(a) (1)-(4).

Pulsifer v.   Comm'r, 64 T.C. 245 (1975)
A father and his three minor children won the Irish sweepstakes. Money was held in trust until children reached 21 years of age or proper application was filed. Taxpayer followed cash method and did not include winnings in his current income.
Held: That since the winnings were set aside in trust and beyond reach of creditors, they had absolute right to winnings. Therefore,

under economic benefit theory, they must include winnings in current year's income.

Minor v. U. S., 772 F.2d 1472 (9th Cir. 1985)
A physician entered into an HMO contract and became a shareholder and director in the corporation. The agreement allowed him to defer a portion of his income over the next 3-4 years until retirement. The deferred income was paid into a trust. IRS claimed that this was an economic benefit that should have been currently taxed.
Held: That compensation deferred was not currently taxable to the employee since the deferred compensation plan was unfunded and the funds were subject to the claims of the corporation's creditors.
2 prong economic benefit test:
  i.   To be currently taxable, an employer's promise must be susceptible of valuation; and
  ii.   There must be no substantial risk of forfeiture to employee because the right is firmly vested in the employee.

Al-Hakim v. Comm'r, 53 T.C.M. 352 (1987).
Taxpayer, a sports agent, was to receive his fee over 10 years in equal installments. The client then made an interest free, unsecured loan to the taxpayer to be repaid over 10 years in the same amounts as the fee owed.
it appeared as though he had income up front.
Held: This was a loan and there was no need to pay the taxes up front as a cash method taxpayer.
The taxpayer was still obligated to pay the loan even though the installments might not be paid. The loan did not offset income received under an installment contract.

Deductions: Reg. § 1.461-1(a)(1)).
The general rule is to take deductions when one pays for a deductible expense. However, if paying creates an asset having a life extending beyond one year, one may have to capitalize.

Comm'r. v. Boyleston Market Association, 131 F.2d 966 (1st Cir. 1942).
Cash method taxpayer purchased 3yr. insurance policy for business. No question that expense qualified as a "business expense," but was it ordinary; i.e., was it a currently deductible item?
Held : Taxpayer obtained "asset" by prepaying insurance; i.e., a set of rights under the insurance contract that would last at least through the three year period of the policy; consequently, taxpayer had to

recover its expenses over the corresponding period and could not deduct the premiums in full at the time they were paid.

2.   Accrual Method.

    a.   The Accrual Method of accounting is used by most businesses
    b.   The key is to match income with the expense of earning that income (Matching Principle).

Under the accrual method of accounting income is to be included for the taxable year when all the events have occurred to **fix** the **right to receive** the income and the **amount** of the income can be determined with **reasonable accuracy.** Under such a method, a liability is incurred and generally is taken into account for Federal Income tax purposes, in the taxable year in which **all the events** have occurred that established the **fact of the liability**, the **amount of** the liability can be determined with reasonable accuracy, and **economic performances** occurred with respect to the liability.

Georgia School Book Depository v. Comm'r, 1 T.C. 463 (1943)
Middleman for a school books company earns a commission from sales to the state. He sent books in 1938 and 1939 however, the state fund was not big enough to make a payment. Middleman fought the claim that he must include the sale as income when sold.
Held: He had to account for the income in 1938 and 1939. He had done everything necessary to claim right to the income, and
there was a reasonable expectation that he would ultimately get paid. If not, he can deduct under IRC § 165.

All Events Test
Income is included in a taxable year when **all events** have occurred to fix the right to receive such income and the amount thereof is determinable with reasonable accuracy.

If there is no "Reasonable anticipation" of getting paid, the right will not accrue and no tax needs to be paid. See Reg. § 1.461-1(a)(2)(ii).

IRC § 455. Prepaid Subscription Income

IRC § 455(a) Prepaid income is included, at the option of the taxpayer, in GI for the taxable years during which the taxpayer's liability to furnish a newspaper, magazine or other periodical exists. IRC §§ 455(a)(1)(c) and (d)(2)

IRC § 455(b) If the liability ends or the taxpayer dies, then all income not yet included will be included in that year.

IRC § 455(c) Only applicable if the taxpayer elects to use this section.

IRC § 455(d) Prepaid subscription income means any amount which is received in connection with, and is directly attributable to, a liability which extends beyond the close of the taxable year and is income from a magazine, newspaper or other periodical. IRC § 455(d)(1).

IRC § 455(d)(2) Liability means a liability to furnish or deliver a periodical.

3.   Installment method: Hybrid of the Cash and Accrual Method.

*   Allows sellers of property who are receiving payment on a deferred basis to pay tax on their gain only as they receive cash from the sale.
*   Allows a taxpayer to delay tax if he is disposing of property and does not have sufficient money to pay the tax on the entire price since he is not paid the entire amount at once.
*   Profit is recognized ratably as payments are made.
*   Only applicable to property sale that earns a gain-not loss and not services

IRC § 453   Installment method

IRC § 453(d) Income from an installment sale is accounted through this method, unless taxpayer otherwise elects.

IRC § 453(b) Installment Sale means the disposition of property where at least one payment is received after the close of the taxable year in which the disposition occurs.

IRC § 453(c) Installment Method is used to determine the ratio of profit to price.

IRC § 453(c)   Divide by "Gross Profit" by "Contract Price"

Example:
Basis = $10,   Sell for $50,   Gross Profit = $40
  "Gross Profit Ratio" = 40/50

Received $4 profit and $1 = nontaxable return of capital (i.e. basis).

IRC § 453(d) Taxpayer can elect out of the installment method

IRC § 453(f)(3) For purposes of the installment method, "payment" may not be accomplished by a promissory note or other evidence of indebtedness of the person acquiring the property, the buyer, regardless of whether TP's debt is guaranteed by a third party, must make an actual payment.

IRC § 456   Prepaid dues income for certain membership organizations

IRC § 456(a) "Prepaid dues income" is included in membership organizations GI for the year in which liability exists.

IRC § 456(e)(2) For purposes of this section "liability" means a liability to render services or make available memberships privileges for a period of time not exceeding 36 months.

IRC § 456(b) Cessation of liability accelerates inclusion of balance of prepaid membership dues income.

American Automobile Assn. v. U.S., 367 U.S. 687 (1961)
Annual dues paid to the AAA were prorated for months the fee covered.
Held: That the income should be recognized when the dues are received.

One can't apportion taxes based on an estimation of when one will earn income since it is dependent on the clients demand.

Artnell Company v. Comm'r, 400 F. 2d 981 (7th Cir 1968)
(Minority view)
Held: That baseball team could defer prepaid season ticket income since the future service was so definite as to allow spreading the income. distinguished on the basis of certainty and the fact that the timing was not at the discretion of the person who paid.

RCA Corp. v. U. S., 664 F.2d 881, (2d Cir. 1981)
RCA sells TV's with service contracts.
RCA wants to spread income from service contracts over the term of the contract to reflect when it would perform services based on estimates.
Held: RCA must include as income when received. It does not matter when events arise because it is problematic to predict a service schedule.

IRC § 461(h) Certain liabilities not incurred before economic performance

All Events test determines which year in which a liability has accrued.

Note:
All events test has been substantially modified by requirement of economic performance. IRC § 461(h)(1) provides that the all events test can not be satisfied any earlier than when "economic performance" has occurred.

* If services or property are provided to the taxpayer, the all events test is not met until the property is actually used or provided to the taxpayer. IRC § 461(h)(2)(A)(i) and (ii) and (iii) relating to use of property by the taxpayer

* If the taxpayer provides goods or services, then it is not met until goods or services are actually provided. IRC § 561(g).

* If paying a tort claim, then no deduction is allowed until payment is actually made.

* Recurring Items deduction can be taken in the year before it would ordinarily be permitted if performance will occur within a reasonable period of time after the close of the year, or within 81/2 months after the close of the year.

U.S. v. General Dynamics Corp., 481 U.S. 239 (1987)
Employer pays for the medical expenses incurred by its employees. At
the end of the year some employees have incurred expenses but not yet
filed claims. Accrual accounting employer can readily predict the
expenses. he wants to deduct these amount at the end of the year, even
though it will not be paid until the following year.
Held: Employer can not deduct in the earlier year because all events had
not occurred.. Filing the claim is the event that triggers the amount
owed and it has not occurred yet.. until the employee files the claim ,
the amount owed is contingent.

Two prong All Events test
     i.   No dispute about the fact that liability has been established
            (legal obligation)
    ii.   The amount of liability can be determined with reasonable
            accuracy

IRC § 464 Limitations on deductions for certain farming expenses

With respect to any "farming syndicate," as defined in IRC § 464(c),
otherwise allowable deductions for feed, seed, fertilizer, or other similar
farm supplies, may only be deducted in the year when they are actually
used and consumed, or if later, the taxable year in which the deduction
would ordinarily be allowed.

The term "farming syndicate" includes a partnership or any other
enterprise (other than a corporation which is not an S corporation
engaged in the trader business of farming), if at any time an interest in
such partnership or enterprise has been offered for sale in any offering
required to be registered with any federal or state agency having authority
to regulate the offering of securities for sale; or if more than 35% of the
losses during any period are allocable to limited partners or limited
entrepreneurs. IRC § 464(c)(1).

Note:
IRC § 464 suppresses the farming shelters where a doctor buys a cow at
the end of the year with a lot of feed that will be used the next year and
then sells it at the beginning of the next year after taking a deduction for
the expenses.

4.   Inventory Accounting.

a.   IRC § 471 General rules for inventory accounting

Inventory method used must conform to best account practice in the trade or business the method that most clearly reflects the income of the taxpayer IRC § 471(a).

General Rules:

*   Inventory is an income producing expenditure. Goods, either finished or partly finished or acquired for sale make up an inventory.

*   A retailer may not simply deduct the cost of inventory purchased during the year. The taxpayer can deduct the cost only if she sells the inventory during the year.

b.   Cost of Goods Sold (CGS).
CGS is calculated at the end of the year by combining the inventory products produced and or purchased during the year plus the inventory on hand at the beginning of the year, once determined. The inventory on hand at the end of the year is subtracted from this figure. The resulting total is the cost of goods sold which is then deducted from annual sales to provide the taxpayer's gross profit.

Inventory is valued under one of the following valuation systems:

c.   LIFO
LIFO means Last In First Out therefore the closing inventory is composed of the earliest purchases (reduces taxes in rising markets);

d.   FIFO
FIFO means First In First Out, therefore the last purchases make up the closing inventory. (this is the preferred method)

*   The inventory value is further calculated under either of two systems;
*   **Cost or Lower of Cost or Market**
*   The method adopted cannot be changed without IRS approval

Example of Inventory Accounting calculation

Beginning Inventory   (is last years ending inventory)
+ Production for year   (includes manufacturing costs direct & indirect)
+ Purchases during year (invoices with transportation costs included)
 Total Inventory for Year
- Ending Inventory for year (Valued Under LIFO (IRC § 472) or FIFO
(at the lower of cost or market))

_____

 Total Cost of Goods Sold

Thor Power Tool Company v. Comm'r, 439 U.S. 522 (1979)
Company had maintained replacement parts, and ended up holding them
for a long time. Based on forecasts, the company began to write down
the excess at once while still keeping parts and selling them at regular
prices. Commissioner disallowed write downs because the procedure did
not reflect income.
Held: Company could not deduct parts as scrap until the parts were
thrown out. Taxpayer could not deduct the amount as long as they were
still selling the parts.

XI. NET OPERATING LOSS, CLAIM OF RIGHT, TAX BENEFITS RULE

Although the impact of taxable transactions is ordinarily determined by the taxpayer's method of accounting within the period of a particular taxable year, at times, events and transactions that take place in one year may have an impact in a subsequent year.

This chapter address three such instances:
A. the Net Operating Loss (NOL) deduction (IRC § 172),
B. the amount deductible when a taxpayer returns an amount previously included in income under a Claim of Right (IRC § 1341); and
C. the so-called Tax Benefit Doctrine which applies where benefits accrue to the taxpayer in one taxable year - typically, by way of a tax deduction - but later events show that the earlier deduction was not justified (IRC § 111).

Ordinarily, when a taxpayer's deductions exceed income, the excess is wasted; i.e., after taxable income in reduced to zero, the taxpayer does not benefit further; i.e., there is no refund. However, in the case of a business taxpayer, the net operating loss forwarded by IRC § 172 may actually permit the taxpayer to reduce its tax liability in earlier (referred to as a *carryback loss*) or *subsequent* (referred to as a *carryforward loss*) taxable years.

A. NET OPERATING LOSS (NOL).

1. Net operating loss deduction: **IRC § 172.**

IRC § 172 (a) An NOL exists when the deductions available to a business taxpayer exceed income. An NOL is defined as ". . . the excess of the [business] deductions allowed . . . over . . . gross income . . . [with adjustments specified in IRC § 172 (d)] (expenses, depreciation, depletion, losses and bad debts) exceed business income

IRC § 172(b) An NOL can be carried back 3 years and carried forward for 15 years. Thus, an NOL can be carried back to each of the three taxable years immediately preceding the taxable year of the NOL and can be carried forward to each of the fifteen taxable years following the year of the NOL. An NOL generates an eighteen-year "window" in which excess business deductions may be utilized. (IRC § 172 (b)). However it must be used in the earliest years possible. Thus, a carryback to the earliest possible year and then carryforward. The taxpayer can choose to waive the carryback period. IRC § 172 (b) (3).

IRC § 172(d) provides that an NOL is calculated by determining the excess of deductions over income:
   a.   without taking into account any net operating loss deduction;
   b.   for noncorporate taxpayers, taxable capital losses are taken into account only to the extent of capital gains (IRC § 172 (d) (2));
   c.   the exclusion provided by IRC § 1202 is not allowed;
   d.   personal exemptions under IRC § 151 are not taken into account (IRC § 172 (d) (3));
   e.   gains attributable to depreciable property used in the trade or business or real property used in the trade or business are treated as ordinary (IRC § 172 (d) (4)); and
   f.   casualty losses are not taken into account.

Burnett v. Sanford & Brooks Co., 228 U.S. 359 (1931)
Taxpayer had a contract with the government that was eventually abandoned. The taxpayer experienced losses which he deducted from his tax return. The government reimbursed him four years later for expenses plus interest. He argued that only the interest was taxable since he made no profits on the deal.
Held: All receipts are part of GI regardless of whether or not they were profitable. Therefore, even if money received is a repayment for past expenses, it is still taxable today.

Note:
IRC § 460, now provides that taxpayers who provide services under long-term contracts, can realize income for the purposes based on the percentage of the work completed each year.

2.   Claim of Right.

   a.   In General

The "Claim of Right" doctrine is essentially tax accounting, i.e., a timing, principle, which provides that a taxpayer must include an item of income in the year in which the item is received unconditionally, even if later events may require the item of income be returned. Although innocuous on its face, it can lead to inequitable results which can be illustrated as follows:

Example 1:
Two cash method (see Chapter IX) taxpayers, A and B, are litigating over a contract claim. A is suing to collect compensation for his services he claims are due him under the contract, while B asserts that A is not entitled to anything, because he breached the contract. If a trial court directs B to pay compensation to A in Year 1, A will have compensation income in that Year, because he *received it*, even if B is later successful on appeal in his argument that A is entitled to nothing due to breach of contract. If B is ultimately successful, A would then have to repay the money previously included.

North American Oil Consolidated v. Burnett, 286 U.S. 417 (1932)
Rule: If a taxpayer (TP) receives money and claims that he is entitled to it and can freely dispose of it, he is taxable in the year of the receipt. The fact that he might have to give it back in later years is disregarded. Thus, if there is money in dispute due to a litigation, as soon as the money is put in a fund and a lower court says that it is TP's, TP has a claim of right and must pay taxes on it in that year.

U.S. v. Lewis, 340 U.S. 590 (1951)
Taxpayer erroneously received a bonus in 1944. (TP had to pay back a portion of the bonus in 1946). While he had it, he treated it as his own money.
Held: That he must treat it as income in 1944, then deduct it as a loss in 1946.
Presumably, the repayment by A in *Example 1* would "balance" A's books; i.e., it would seem to offset the erroneous (as it turned out) inclusion of compensation in the earlier year; but would it?

Example 2:
Assume the same facts as in previous example, except that A was a 50% taxpayer (marginal rate) in the earlier year in which the compensation was turned over to him unconditionally, but only in the 15% marginal bracket in the year of repayment. In retrospect, the "inclusion" cost him 50% of every dollar received, but the repayment generated tax savings of only 15%.

b. Claim of Right: In Detail.

Claim of Right is essentially a relief measure that addresses situations such as A's. It is codified in IRC § 1341, which provides that where:

  i.   taxpayer previously included an item in income, because received under an unrestricted Claim of Right; and

  ii. the taxpayer is entitled to a deduction for the current taxable year, because it turned out - after the close of the prior year - that he did not have such a right and the amount has been repaid; and

  iii. The deduction exceeds $3,000, the taxpayer's tax for the year of repayment is the *lower of*

     A) "her tax liability for the taxable year computed with the deduction; or

     B) her tax liability computed *without* the deduction, *reduced by* "the decrease in tax . . . for the prior taxable year . . . which would result . . . from the exclusion of the income item from gross income for such prior taxable year . . . ."

Example 3:

Facts are same as in previous examples, except that IRC § 1341 is applicable. A's liability for the year of repayment would be reduced by 50% of the amount repaid; i.e., the additional tax in the prior year attributable to the amount included under Claim of Right.

3. Tax Benefit Rule.

    a. In General

The Tax Benefit rule generally applies when a taxpayer has deducted an item in an earlier taxable year, which is "recovered" in a subsequent taxable year. Such a situation might occur, for example, where a taxpayer deducts a medical expense in the year in which the medical expense is actually paid, and reimbursement is received in a subsequent taxable year. The "recovery" or other "inconsistent" event requires taxpayer to offset the earlier year tax benefit by including the amount previously deducted in income for her taxable year in which recovery takes place.

b.   Recovery of tax benefit items (no choice): IRC §111.

GI does not include income received which represents recovery of an item that was deducted in a previous year so long as no tax benefit was received in the prior year.

Must take NOL carryforwards and backs into account

Alice Phelan Sullivan Corporation v. U.S.,   381 F. 2d 399 (Ct Cl. 1967)
T gave the city a building as a charitable contribution and proceeded to deduct the FMV. The city later returned the building.
Held: The return is income in the year it was received. The taxpayer must pay tax at the rate at the time of recovery. The amount of tax savings in the earlier year is irrelevant.

XII. DEPLETION

A. DEPLETION: IN GENERAL

The IRC permits a reasonable allowance for depletion. In the case of mines, oil wells, gas, other natural deposits and timber. Due to the fact that the allowance computed with regard to "wasting" assets, a computation of the allowance is somewhat different in that for depreciation. The purpose of the allowance is to permit the owner of an economic interest in a wasting asset to recover his/her investment during the period in which the exhaustion occurs.

B. DEPLETION IN DETAIL

1. Allowance of deduction for depletion: **IRC § 611**

The method for computing the deduction for depletion may be computed on the basis of the taxpayer's cost for the natural resource ("cost depletion") or with regard to the amount of income for the property ("percentage depletion"). IRC §§ 612; 613; 613(A)

2. Basis cost depletion: **IRC § 612**

Cost depletion involves the recovery by way of depletion deductions from the taxpayer's basis in the property. IRC § 612 provides that the taxpayer's basis for this purpose is the adjusted basis provided by IRC § 1011 for the purposes of determining gain or loss on the sale or other disposition of property.

Reg § 1.611-2(a) provides that the calculation of cost depletion involves 3 variables:
    i.   the taxpayer's adjusted basis in the property as of the beginning of   the taxable year;
    ii. the number of units of natural resource property as of the beginning of the year; and
    iii. the number of units sold within the taxable year.

3. Computation of cost depletion.

Is provided by dividing the taxpayer's basis in the property as of the beginning of the taxable year and by multiplying the "depletion unit," thus calculated, by the number of units sold during the taxable year. A "unit" is the principal or customary unit in which resource property is sold. The term might include tons or ore, barrels of oil, cubic feet of natural gas etc. Reg. § 1.611-2(a)(1).

Note:
As with depreciation, the allowance for depletion causes the taxpayer's basis in the mineral property to be reduced IRC § 1016(a)(2).

4. Percentage depletion: **IRC § 613.**

The allowance for percentage depletion is substantially different than the allowance for cost depletion. The latter is calculated on the basis of the taxpayer's investment in the mineral property. In contrast, percentage depletion represents a percentage - specified by statute - from the taxpayer's gross income from the mineral property.

Except in specified circumstances, the taxpayer is permitted to use cost depletion or percentage depletion, which ever produces the larger allowance. However, percentage depletion is generally not available for determining depletion in oil and gas investments, except as provided in IRC § 613(A); and investors in timber may not use cost depletion. Reg § 1.611-1(a).

5. Depletion Pertaining to Oil, Gas and Mineral Producers.

   a. Repeal of percentage depletion for oil and gas producers.

   IRC § 613(A) provides, in substance, that the allowance for percentage depletion is no longer available for taxable use beginning after 1974 for domestic and foreign oil and gas production. However, exceptions exist for regulated natural gas, certain geothermal deposits and natural gas sold under a fixed contract (IRC §§ 613(A)(b), 613 (A)(c).

b.   Eligibility For Depletion: Economic Interests In Mineral.

In general, to be eligible for a depletion allowance with respect to mineral property, the taxpayer must have some "economic interest" in the property.
Reg. § 1.611-1(b)(2) provides that an economic interest is possessed where ". . . taxpayer has acquired by investment any interest in any mineral in place or standing timber, and secures, by any form of legal relationship, income derived from the extraction of the mineral or severance of the timber, to which he must look for a return on his/her capital . . . ." The regulation observes that the mere right to purchase or process a product upon production does not convey a depletable economic interest. The acquisition "by investment " includes gifts and inheritances and they encompass retained economic interests in mineral property disposed of by the taxpayer, unless there has been "a sale" of timber, coal or domestic iron ore under IRC § 631(b) or IRC § 631(c).

c.   Intangible Drilling Expenses in Oil and Gas.
IRC § 263(c) Intangible drilling expenses in oil, gas and geothermal wells. Notwithstanding the general requirement that capital expenditures be added to basis and recovered only by way of depreciation, amortization or depletion,

IRC §263(c) affords the taxpayer the option of treating certain expenses, such as those for wages, supplies, site location and preparation for production and drilling as either currently deductible expenses or capital expenditures. If the latter course is chosen, the taxpayer's basis in the depletable property is larger and more may be recovered by way of cost depletion. In contrast, if the taxpayer has a high income production from the mineral property, it may be advisable to take advantage of percentage depletion, which is not hampered by the taxpayer's low cost basis.

Expenses to which the option relates include expenditures "incident to and necessary for the drilling of wells and the preparation of wells in the production of oil and gas." Thus, the cost of drilling and development, including expenditures for supplies, repairs, fuel and labor, should be within the scope of IRC § 263(c), Reg. § 1.612-4(a).

XIII. TAX SHELTERS

A. DEFERRAL/CONVERSION: IN GENERAL.

Tax shelters attempt to achieve either deferral of the realization of income or the conversion of ordinary income to capital gain, or both.

1. Deferral.
Deferral consists of pushing income into the future by incurring costs that are currently deductible and realizing the corresponding return from the investment in some future year. The tax advantage arises from the use of the funds ("time value" of money concept) that would otherwise be paid in taxes for the period of deferral.

2. Conversion.
Conversion consists of converting ordinary income into tax favored income, usually by taking deductions against ordinary income for the costs of investments that produce tax-exempt income, tax-free loans on the security of property with unrealized appreciation, or capital gain.

B. TAX SHELTERS: IN DETAIL

1. The Classic Tax Shelter: An Illustration.

IRC § 183(b) provides that no deductions on " not for profit activities" shall be allowed except as provided:
- i.   for the deduction for real property taxes, which are allowable without regard to whether or not the activity is engaged in for profit;
- ii.   a deduction for a portion of " not for profit expenses", but only to the extent that they equal the gross income derived form the activity, reduced by "otherwise allowable" deductions whether or not the activity was engaged in for profit.

IRC § 183(d) establishes a presumption that if the not for profit activity has generated positive income for three or more of the taxable years in the five taxable years immediately preceding the taxable year for which the deduction is sought, the activity will be presumed to have been engaged in for profit.

Note: with a not for profit activity that relates to breeding, training, showing, or racing of horses, this period is extended to seven years, but the taxpayer need only to show profits in two of the seven years.

Example:
T buys a building with borrowed funds. In year one, he collects $3,000 rent which is treated as ordinary income; he pays $500 in mortgage interest under (IRC § 163), deductible property taxes of $1,000 (IRC § 164), deductible utilities and maintenance expenses of $1,000 (IRC § 162) and depreciation of $1,000 (IRC §§ 167, 168).

This example illustrates that the taxpayer can have a positive cash flow "income of $ *"less* deductible out of pocket expenses $ = cash flow", but nonetheless shows a deductible loss due to the depreciation deduction.

2. Losses From Investments In Property And The Savings And Loan (S&L) Crisis.

In the 1980's, Savings and Loans Associations ("S&L's"), as an industry, experienced severe financial strains. Many S&Ls held long-term mortgages at low interest rates. To stay in business, however, they were forced to borrow at high rates, the resulting "squeeze" forced many S&Ls out of business. S&Ls sought a way to obtain tax benefits from their mortgage portfolios to mitigate their economic losses. In some cases, the plan adopted included so-called "mortgage swaps". In theory, these swaps were taxable events which permitted the S&Ls to realize and recognize huge tax losses without substantially altering their asset portfolios.

In *Cottage Savings And Loan Association v. Comm'r.,* 499 U.S. 554 (1991),
The court determined that a financial institution experiences a tax deductible loss when it exchanges its interest in one group in one residential loans for the residential loans of another mortgage lender, only if the debts exchanged are materially different. Because the loans were different obligors and secured by different properties, exchanged interests did embody legally distinct entitlements. Consequently, the taxpayer realized its losses at the time of the swap of the mortgage pools.

Example:
S&L #1 has $100,000 mortgage at 3%. Interest rates go to up to 6% and mortgage is now worth only $50,000. Swaps at $50,000 with S&L #2 and each takes a $50,000 loss, but keeps the mortgage on their books at $100,000.

3.   Qualified Pensions.

Generally, to prevent abuses of people dumping inordinate amounts of money into tax deferred pensions, Congress has limited the types of pension plans that are permitted favorable tax treatment.

IRC § 401   Qualified Pension, profit sharing and stock bonus plans (the last great tax shelter)

IRC § 401(a) Requirements for a plan in order to qualify for tax benefits:
  (a)(5) Non-discrimination requirements include no discrimination of employees based on salary; contributions to plans must bear a uniform relationship to compensation, etc.
  (a)(7) Non-forfeitable requirement that plans must vest after a certain period of time
  (a)(11) The interest of the employee's spouse must be part of the plan

IRC § 401(b) Retroactive changes

IRC § 401(c) Qualifications for plans relating to self-employed individuals and owners-employees

IRC § 401(k) Employees are not taxed on amounts greater than, or equal to $7,000 per year put aside for retirement even if they had the option to take cash; employers can immediately deduct amounts paid into the plan; earnings on funds paid into the plan and invested by it are not taxed to employees until withdrawn.

4. Individual Retirement Accounts (IRAs).

    a. Individual retirement accounts: **IRC § 408**
IRC § 408(a) Taxpayer can place up to $2,000 into an individual retirement plan (IRA) which has similar tax benefits on interest earned as if under IRC § 401.

    b. Effect of the "1997 Act"

Under the law as it existed prior to August 5, 1997, taxpayers were permitted to contribute up to $2,000 (and in some instances more than $2,000) to an individual retirement account. The principle advantages of this account consisted of:
(1) a deduction for the contribution, unless the taxpayer was disqualified either because of income or participation in a qualified pension plan; and
(2) a deferral of tax on the amount contributed to the IRA until it was withdrawn. The "1997 Act" enhances these benefits in several important respects. First, in 1998, taxpayers will be permitted to contribute up to $500 "for each beneficiary" under the age of 18. Contributions may be made to a custodial account created to pay the beneficiary's educational costs, certain kinds of trust or "an education savings account."
It is important to note that contributions to a qualified account for trust should also qualify for the annual exclusion for gift taxes under IRC § 2503. As with individual retirement accounts, the earnings of the account are not taxed until withdrawal. However, any earnings which are not used to pay the beneficiaries educational expenses are subject to a penalty.

A second quite important benefit created under the "1997 Act" is the so-called "Roth IRA." In effect, the "Roth IRA" permits the taxpayer to dodge the tax which would ordinarily apply to when previously exempt funds held in an IRA are distributed.

c.   Roth IRA.
In a nutshell, the "1997 Act" provides the following new account options:
"Roth IRA"
- (1) Contributions are not tax deductible
- (2) Earnings are tax-free after five years
- (3) Eligibility phases out for upper bracket taxpayer:
  Couples $150,000 to $160,000
  Individuals $ 95,000 to $110,000
- (4) Raises income limits (gradually) for those eligible to make tax-deductible contributions to traditional IRAs:
  Full contribution for couples to $80,000 from $40,000
  Full contribution for singles to $50,000 from $25,000
- (5) Penalty free withdrawals before age 591/2 for educational purposes
- (6) Penalty free withdrawals before age 591/2 for first-time home buyers

d.   Education Savings

IRA for education for parents under certain income levels:
- (1) Contributions up to $500 per child
  Contributions are not tax-free.
  Earnings are not taxed.
- (2) Must be withdrawn by the time child is age 30

	Roth Ira	**Traditional IRA**
Maximum Annual ContributionH	$2,000	$2,000
Who Is Eligible	Anyone with earned income below $110,000 (single) $160,000 (joint)	Anyone under age 70 _ with earned income, no matter how much
	2,000 contribution allowance phases out between $95,000 to $110,000 (single), to $160,000 (joint) Non-working spouses can contribute up to $2,000	Non-working spouses can contribute up to $2,000

	Roth Ira	**Traditional IRA**
Tax Deductibility Of Contributions	Not tax deductible	Deductibility of contribution is based on th modified adjusted gross income for the 1998 tax year of $30,000-$40,000 (single), $50,000-$60,000 (joint). These levels will increase over the next 10 years Beginning in the 1998 tax year, if both spouses work an one is not covered by a employer plan, non-covere spouse can deduct contribution (adjusted gros income less than $160,00(with deductibility phased out for AGI's between $150,000 and $160,000.
Withdrawal Of Assets	Can withdraw earnings free from General income tax if account has been open for 5 years plus any of the following: age 59 _ , purchase of first home ($10,000 lifetime cap), permanent disability, or death).	Withdrawals can be made penalty-free before age 59 for purchase of first-time home or higher education (taxes apply on earnings withdrawn) Certain withdrawals made prior to age 59 _ may be subject to an additional 10% penalty tax
Rollovers And Transfers	Can roll over to a Traditional IRA to a Roth IRA (adjusted gross income no more than $100,000; money is subject to taxation)	Can transfer to and from other Traditional IRAs Can roll over from employer plans (i.e., 401(k)s)

Combined maximum contribution to both Roth IRA and Traditional = $2,000

C. ANTI-TAX SHELTER PROVISIONS

1. Restriction on investment interest: **IRC § 163(d).**

* Excess is not currently deductible.
* However, it may be carried forward and deducted against investment income in future taxable years.
* This does not apply to interest incurred in carrying on a trade or business.

2. Capitalization Requirement: **IRC § 263A**

* Requires taxpayer to capitalize all indirect and direct costs of producing property.
* This prevents immediate deductions of such costs.

3. Not For Profit Activities (Hobby Losses): **IRC § 183**

* Demands profit motive for "personal" expenses, i.e. those losses not incurred in a trade or business are disallowed.

4. Deduction limited to amount at risk: **IRC § 465**

IRC § 465 (b)(2) provides that the taxpayer is "at risk" with respect to debt used in an activity, only if ;
    a. he is personally liable for the repayment of the debt ; or
    b. has pledged property as security for the amount of the debt.

Note:

This section applies to individual taxpayers and C corporations which are "closely held" as defined in IRC § 542(a)(2) (relating to personal holding companies).
* Focuses in on concept of non-recourse debt.
* Defines the amount considered to be at risk = money contributed (down payment) and loans that are RECOURSE
* Allows for an indefinite carry-over of loss until one has money at risk. (Loss carry-over is not included in Net Operating Loss)
* IRC § 465(b)(6) -- loophole for qualified nonrecourse loans

Example: IRC § 465
T Produces movie and borrows $550,000 (non-recourse)
put up $ 50,000 (at risk)
If 1st year income is $150,000
and deduction are $400,000.
Then $250,000 is the excess deduction over income
However, only the at risk amount of $50,000 can be deducted and
$200,000 can be carried over until T puts more money up at Risk, or
carry forward can be taken upon sale.

5.   Alternative Minimum Tax (AMT).

    a.   AMT In General

    The ultimate Anti-Tax Shelter Provision: IRC §§ 55, 56, 57, 58.
    If triggered, one must pay the larger amount.

    TP must do tax return computation twice, and if amount under
    AMT is greater, TP must pay that amount.

    AMT (alternative minimum tax) imposes a tax to ensure that a
    taxpayer does not take advantage of certain preferences or deductions
    to avoid all taxes.

    The taxpayer pays resulting tax from the AMT to the extent that it
    exceeds the normal tax.

    AMT is usually lower because although taxable income is greater.
    the
     tax rates are lower

    MINIMUM TAX CREDIT = the extent that the AMT tax
    attributable to timing rules (as opposed to exclusions, i.e., interest)
    exceeds the regular tax credits which can be bottled to use in
    subsequent years to reduce any excess of regular tax over AMT

    Where the taxpayer is subject to an Alternative Minimum Tax
    (AMT) in calculation in IRC § 55 and has taken depreciation
    deductions in computing *regular tax liability*, the taxpayer's
    alternative minimum taxable income- in general - by using longer
    periods produces lower deductions and higher AMT.   In some cases,
    the 1997 Act liberalizes the AMT provisions in favor or the

taxpayers in industries that have intensive demands on capital and certain "small business corporations."

b. Alternative minimum tax imposed: IRC §55

IRC §55 lists exemption amounts, which serves to get the majority of the population *out of the AMT* plan..

IRC § 55(a) AMT = excess tentative minimum tax (TMT) over the regular tax

IRC 55(b)(1) TMT = 26% of taxable excess greater than or equal to $175,000 ($87,500 m/f/s) and 28% for taxable excess greater than $175,000 for a taxpayer other than a corporation (Corporate rate = 20%)

IRC § 55(b)(1)(A)(ii) Taxable excess = excess of the alternative minimum taxable income over exemptions

IRC § 55(b)(2) AMT income = taxable income determined with adjustments under IRC §§56 and 58 and increased by the amount of preference items under IRC § 57

IRC § 55(c) Regular tax = regular tax liability reduced by certain credits allowed under AMT

IRC § 55(d)(1) Non-corporate exemption are: joint/surviving spouse = $45,000; single = $33,750; trust/estate/married filing separate = $22,500

IRC § 55(d)(2) Corporate exemptions = $40,000

IRC § 55(d)(3) Exemptions shall be reduced (not greater than 0) by 25% of AMT income That exceeds $150,000 = joint/surviving/corporation; $112,500 = single; $75,000 = trust/estate/married filing separately.

IRC 55(d)(3)(C) In the case of a married filing separately, AMT income is increased by the lessor of $22,500 or 25% of excess AMT income (determined without regard for the provision) over $165,000

c.   Adjustments in computing alternative minimum taxable income: IRC § 56

Provides changes in deductibility specifying items that affect both the individual and, or the corporation

The calculation of the AMT amount:

AGI + certain tax preferences (certain contributions, medical expenses in excess of 10% of AGI, wagering losses, interest, some depreciation) and then subtracting the exemption amount. This amount is taxed at 21%. If this amount exceeds taxpayer's regular tax, taxpayer must pay AMT.

IRC § 56(a) Adjustments applicable to *all taxpayers* include depreciation of real/personal property: intangible drilling costs; % completion, etc.

IRC § 56(b) Adjustments applicable *to individuals only* include state/local taxes under IRC § 164; medical expenses under IRC § 213 must exceed 10% AGI rather than 7.5%; incentive stocks; research and development; passive losses; itemized deductions, etc.

IRC § 56(c) Adjustments applicable *to corporations only* include bad debt reserves, etc.

d.   Items of tax preference: IRC § 57.

IRC § 57(a) Preferences include depletion; intangible drilling costs; reserves for losses bad debts; tax exempt interest; appreciated property charitable deductions

e.   Denial of certain losses: IRC § 58

IRC § 58(a) Disallowance of certain farm tax shelter losses

IRC § 58(b) Disallowance of passive activity losses

IRC § 58(c) Special rules for insolvent taxpayers are defined

XIV. LITIGATION WITH THE IRS

A. LEGISLATIVE DEVELOPMENT: THE 1998 ACT.

1. The Taxpayer Restructuring and Reform Act of 1998: The 1998 Act.

The most significant legislative development during 1998-9 was the enactment of the 1998 Act.

The 1998 Act:
- a. shifts the burden of proof to the government on certain factual issues;
- b. allows an individual taxpayer to apply non-refundable personal credits, such as the HOPE credit and the Lifetime Learning Credit, which are geared to higher education expenses, against his/her regular tax liability during 1998;
- c. permits an individual to deduct interest on a "qualified education loan;" (4) permits a prize winner to avoid constructive receipt of a prize if what he/she receives is a "qualified prize option;"
- d. provides that by the year 2003, those who are self-employed will be able to deduct 100% of their health insurance costs;
- e. modifies the net operating loss (NOL) carryback rules for certain types of losses; and
- f. expands the availability of the deduction for casualty and theft losses.

2. Shift of Burden of Proof.

The 1998 legislation enacts a new section of the Internal Revenue Code (IRC § 7491), which provides that if certain criteria are satisfied, the burden of proof shifts to the Government on any "factual issue relevant to ascertaining the income tax liability of a taxpayer."

- a. The criteria that must be met before the burden of proof shifts include the following:
    - i. The taxpayer must assert a position based on "credible evidence" with respect to a specific factual issue;

    - ii. The taxpayer must have "cooperated" with the IRS and the Department of the Treasury concerning the relevant issue including compliance, with all "reasonable requests" for access to witnesses, meetings and interviews, relevant information, and requests to inspect documents within the control of the taxpayer; and

iii. The taxpayer is an individual or a corporation, partnership or trust (other than a qualified revocable trust" as defined in IRC § 645(b)(1)) described in IRC §7430(c)(4)(A)(ii). That is, the taxpayer's net worth at the time the action was filed was not in excess of $7 million and it had no more than 500 employees.

Note: (1) the question of who has the burden of proof with respect to a particular question is to be resolved on an issue by issue basis; and
(2) the taxpayer retains the burden of substantiating, i.e., establishing
by written evidence, any item set forth in his/her/its return: IRC § 7491(a)(1)(C).

TABLE OF CASES

Al-Hakim v. Comm'r 178
Alice Phelan Sullivan Corporation v. U.S. 191
Allen v. Comm'r 159
American Automobile Assn. v.U.S. 181
Arkansas Best v. Comm'r 131
Armantrout v. Comm'r 18
Artnell Company v. Comm'r 182
Benaglia v. Comm'r 7
Biedenharn Realty v. U.S. 131
Blackman v. Comm'r 77
Blair v. Comm'r 159
Bob Jones v. U.S. 173
Brooke v. U.S. 167
Burnett v. Sanford & Brooks Co 188
Carroll v. Comm'r 71, 83
Cohan v. Comm'r 85
Comm'r v. Boyleston Market Association 178
Comm'r v. Indianapolis Power and Light 21
Comm'r v. Soliman 74
Comm'r. v. Tufts 28
Commissioner v. Duberstein 24
Corn Products Refining v. Comm'r 131
Cottage Savings And Loan Association V. Comm'r. 198
Culbertsonv. Comm'r 170
Danville Plywood Corp. v. Comm'r 88
Diedrich v. Comm'r 38
Dyer v. Comm'r 77
Encyclopedia Britannica v. Comm'r 69
Flowers v. Comm'r 89
Fogelsong v. Comm'r 172
Georgia School Book Depository v. Comm'r 179
Giannini v. Comm'r 157
Gilbert v. Commissioner 20
Gilliam v. Comm'r 70
Glenshaw Glass, Co. v. Comm'r 5
Hantzis v. Comm'r 89
Harrison v. Schaffner 159
Heim v. Fitzpatrick 159
Helvering v. Eubank 158
Helvering v. Horst 157
Henderson v. Comm'r 87

Hort v. Comm'r...147
Hotel Sulgrave v. Comm'r...............................77
Hundley v. Comm'r...159
INDOPCO v. Comm'r................................51, 70
Johnson v. Comm'r...173
Jordan Marsh v. Comm'r................................138
Kirby Lumber v. U.S.......................................37
Levine v. Comm'r..87
Lucas v. Earl..156
M.L. Eakes v. Comm'r....................................71
McAllister v. Comm'r....................................148
Midland Empire Packing Company v. Comm'r....69
Miller v. Comm'r..148
Minor v. U. S...178
Moller v. U.S..74
Morris v. Comm'r..77
Moss v. Comm'r..87
Newark Star Morning Ledger Co. v. U.S.........63
Nickerson v. Comm'r.......................................92
North American Oil Consolidated v. Burnett......189
Ochs v. Comm'r...80
Old Colony Trust Co. v. Comm'r......................5
Ottawa Sillica v. U.S......................................97
Pevsner v. Comm'r..81
Poe v. Seaborn...158
Pulsifer v. Comm'r...177
RCA Corp v. U. S...182
Rudolph v U.S...87
Sargent v. Comm'r..172
Schlier v. Comm'r..41
Schultz v. Comm'r...87
Schuster v. Comm'r...98
Simon v. Comm'r...60
Smith v. Comm'r..124
South Carolina v. Baker...................................44
Starker v. U.S..135
Stephens v. Comm'r...39
Taft v. Bowers..32
Taylor v. Comm'r..80
Teschner v. Comm'r...19
Thor Power Tool Company v. Comm'r.............185
Times v. Mirror...77
U.S. v. Davis...107

U.S. v. Basye 170
U.S. v. Burke 41
U.S. v. General Dynamics Corp. 183
U.S. v. Gilmore 81
U.S. v. Gotcher 6
U.S. v. Lewis... 189
Van Suetendale v. Comm'r 130
Welch v. Helvering..71
Woodsam Associates, Inc. v. Comm'r............................30
Woodward v. Comm'r...51
Zarin v. Comm'r...37

INDEX

A

Above-The-Line" Deductions..110
Accelerated Cost Recovery System (ACRS) 56
Accession to wealth...5
Accident or health insurance - amounts received...................................42
Accounting Methods...175
Accrual Method Accounting 176
Accrual Method Accounting All Events Test 179
Accrual Method, Accounting 179
Activities not engaged in for profit 90
Adjusted gross income defined..110
Adjustments to basis..29
Alimony and separate maintenance payments...98
Alternative Minimum Tax (AMT)..204
Alternative minimum tax imposed..205
Alternative Minimum Tax, Calculation of 206
Alternative Minimum Tax, Denial of certain losses 206
Alternative Minimum Tax, Items of tax preference 206
Alternative minimum taxable income, adjustments imposed............................206
Amortization of goodwill and other intangibles......................................62
Annuity...33
Anti-Tax Shelter Provisions..203
Anti-tax Shelter, Capitalization Requirement.......................................203
Anti-tax Shelter, Deduction limited..203
Anti-tax Shelter, restriction on investment interest 203
Anti-tax ShelterNot For Profit Activities..203
Applicable convention...57
Applicable depreciation methods...56
Applicable recovery period 57
Arbitrage bonds...47

B

Bargain Sales - charitable deduction..97
Basis of property...31
Basis property...135
Below-the-line" deductions 112
Bonds used to pay tuition...44
Boot, paid/received..136
Business Associations 169

Business expenses 66

C

Calculation of basis..29
Camps 7
Capital Assets defined 125
Capital Expenditures..50
Capital Gain..146
Capital Gain Or Ordinary Income 147
Capital loss carrybacks 151
Capital loss carryovers 151
Capital losses, limitations 151
Capitalization and inclusion in inventory costs of certain expenditures.......51
Cash Method Accounting..176
Cash Method of accounting, Limitations 171
Cash Method, Accounting..176
Cash Method Rules 177
Certain death benefits...15
Certain exchanges of insurance policies 144
Charitable contribution deduction 95
Charitable remainder trust 163
Child support - GI..98
Claim of right 188
Clifford Doctrine 165
Clothing expense deduction..80
Compensation for injuries or sickness......................................40
Computation of taxable income 109
Cash Method Rules 177
Contribution Base 95
Convenience of the employer.. 6
Corporations 171
Corporations, Allocation of income and deductions...................172
Corporations, tax imposed 171
Cosmetic surgery expense..79
Cost of Goods Sold 184

D

De minimis fringe...11
Death..15
Dependent defined 121
Depletion...193, 194
Depletion allowance, Economic Interest....................................195
Depletion deduction, allowance for...193

Depletion, Basis cost 193
Depletion, Intangible drilling expenses 195
Depletion, Percentage 194
Depletion, Repeal of percentage 194
Depletion, Repeal of percentage for oil and gas 194
Depreciation 54
Discharge of indebtedness 35
Distributable net income 162
Double declining balance 59

E

Earned income credit 122
Education 81
Education deductible 70
Education Savings 201
Election to expense certain depreciable assets 61
Employer provided health care 43
Entertainment expense, Disallowance of 84
Entertainment expense, Disallowance of certain 84
Entertainment Tickets 86
Estates and trusts accumulating income
    or distributing corpus, deduction for 163
Exchange of property held for productive use or investment ... 133
Exclusion for gains on small business - 50% 153
Exempt facility bond 46
Exemptions 118
Expenditure 49
Expense 49

F

Farming expenses, Limitations on deductions 183
FIFO 184
Foreign conventions 85

G

Gain from dispositions of certain depreciable property 132
Gain from dispositions of certain depreciable realty,
    gain from dispositions 132
Gift, bequest, devise or inheritance 23
Goodwill 71
Grantor Trust, administrative powers 166
Grantor Trust, income for benefit of grantor 166
Grantor Trust, person (not grantor) treated as substantial owner ... 166

Grantor Trust, power to control beneficial enjoyment............................165
Grantor Trust, power to revoke 166
Grantor Trusts 163
Grantor Trusts, definitions and rules..165
Gross Income 3
Group term life insurance purchased for employees 14

H

Home office 72
Household with qualified dependents..123

I

Illegal income..39
Imputed income 22
Income, Definition of... 3
Income Derived From Property 157
Income derived from property community property state 158
Income derived from services or property...158
Individual Retirement Aaccount, Roth...201
Individual Retirement Account - EducationalSavings...........................201
Individual Retirement Accounts (IRA)...200
Installment method Accounting..180
Installment Method Accounting, Prepaid dues income for certain membership
    organizations...181
Intangible property - amortization...55
Interest..93
Interest on state or local bonds..43
Inventory Accounting calculation 185
Inventory, FIFO..184
Inventory, LIFO..184
Involuntary conversions...142
IRC § 1.. 3
IRC § 11...171
IRC § 21...123
IRC § 32...122
IRC § 55...205
IRC § 56...206
IRC § 57...206
IRC § 58...206
IRC § 61 ....10, 21, 22
IRC § 61(a)(1):..3, 13
IRC § 61(a)(3)...25
IRC § 61(a)(8)...98

IRC § 61(a)(12) 35
IRC § 62 110
IRC § 63 ....3, 111
IRC § 63(e) 112
IRC § 67 113
IRC § 68 113
IRC § 71 99
IRC § 72 34
IRC § 72(a) 34
IRC § 72(b) 34
IRC § 72(b)(3)(A) 34
IRC § 72(b)(3)(B) 35
IRC § 72(b)(3)(C) 34
IRC § 72(c) 35
IRC § 72(c)(3)(C) 35
IRC § 74 24
IRC § 79(a) 14
IRC § 83 16
IRC § 83(c)(1) 17
IRC § 83(c)(2) 17
IRC § 85 22
IRC § 86 21
IRC § 86(a)(2) 21
IRC § 101 ....15, 16
IRC § 101(a)(1) 15
IRC § 101(a)(1); 15
IRC § 101(a)(2) 15
IRC § 101(c) 16
IRC § 101(2) 29
IRC § 101(4) 29
IRC § 102 23
IRC § 102(a) 23
IRC § 102(b) 23
IRC § 102(c) 24
IRC § 103(a) 43
IRC § 103(b) 44
IRC § 104 40
IRC § 104(a)(2) 40
IRC § 104(a)(3)) 42
IRC § 104(a)(3)). 42
IRC § 104(a): 40
IRC § 105 42
IRC § 105(a) 42

IRC § 105(b)..42
IRC § 105(h)..43
IRC § 106 43
IRC § 107 ....7, 25
IRC § 108 35
IRC § 108(1)(3)...36
IRC § 108(a)(1) 36
IRC § 108(a)(1)(B) 36
IRC § 108(a)(1)(c)(g) 36
IRC § 108(a)(3)) 36
IRC § 108(d)(1)(a),(b). 37
IRC § 108(d)(3)) 36
IRC § 108(g)..36
IRC § 111 191
IRC § 117 ....24, 81, 82
IRC § 119 6
IRC § 119(a).. 6
IRC § 119(a)(1) 13
IRC § 119(b).. 6
IRC § 119(c).. 7
IRC § 119(d).. 7
IRC § 119(d)(2)) 7
IRC § 121 141
IRC § 127 82
IRC § 132 ....8, 9
IRC § 132(1)..11
IRC § 132(j)(1)...9
IRC § 132(a).. 8
IRC § 132(a)(2) 14
IRC § 132(b)..10
IRC § 132(b)(1)...9, 13
IRC § 132(c)..11
IRC § 132(d)..11
IRC § 132(e)..11
IRC § 132(e)(2) 12
IRC § 132(f)..12
IRC § 132(g)..12
IRC § 132(g)..12
IRC § 132(l) 9
IRC § 135 44
IRC § 141 45
IRC § 141(b)..45
IRC § 141(d)..46

IRC § 141(e)(1) 45
IRC § 143 46
IRC § 144 46
IRC § 145 46
IRC § 146 46
IRC § 148 47
IRC § 149 47
IRC § 151 ....3, 120
IRC § 152 ....3, 121
IRC § 162 ....6, 11, 39, 66
IRC § 162(c), (f) and (g), ...39
IRC § 163 93
IRC § 163(d) 203
IRC § 164 94
IRC § 165 75
IRC § 165(d) 38
IRC § 165(g) 148
IRC § 167 ....11, 54
IRC § 168 55
IRC § 170 95
IRC § 172 187
IRC § 179 61
IRC § 183(b) 197
IRC § 195 53
IRC § 197 62
IRC § 212 72
IRC § 213 79
IRC § 215 99
IRC § 217 12
IRC § 263 49
IRC § 263A 51, 203
IRC § 263(c) 195
IRC § 265 47
IRC § 274(j). 25
IRC § 274(m). 6
IRC § 280A 72
IRC § 280E 39, 75
IRC § 401 199
IRC § 408 200
IRC § 441 175
IRC § 448 171
IRC § 453 180
IRC § 455 180

IRC § 456 181
IRC § 464 183
IRC § 465 203
IRC § 469 78
IRC § 471 184
IRC § 482 172
IRC § 501 173
IRC § 611 193
IRC § 612 193
IRC § 613 194
IRC § 641 161
IRC § 643 162
IRC § 644 162
IRC § 651 162
IRC § 661 163
IRC § 662 163
IRC § 671 164
IRC § 672 165
IRC § 673 165
IRC § 674 165
IRC § 675 166
IRC § 676 166
IRC § 678 166
IRC § 701 169
IRC § 702 169
IRC § 703 169
IRC § 704 170
IRC § 1001 .... 25, 148
IRC § 1014 31
IRC § 1014(b)(9) 31
IRC § 1015 32
IRC § 1015(d)(6) 33
IRC § 1016 29
IRC § 1031 133
IRC § 1033 142
IRC § 1034 139
IRC § 1035 144
IRC § 1041 106
IRC § 1045 153
IRC § 1091 78
IRC § 1202 153
IRC § 1211 151
IRC § 1212 151

IRC § 1221..125
IRC § 1222..149
IRC § 1231..128
IRC § 1245..132
IRC § 1250..132
IRC § 1366..171
Itemized Deductions...112
Itemized deductions, overall limitations 113

J

Joint return, tax imposed 119
Joint returns, filing...109

K

Kiddie Tax 115

L

Leasehold Interests...147
Legal Fees deduction..81
LIFO 184
Like kind 134
Like kind exchange of property 135
Limitation rule - gifted property..33
Limitations on depreciation..54
Loans...20
Lodging furnished by educational institutions 7
Long-term/Short term capital gains and losses 149
Loss, Insurance company..75

M

Materiality test - passive activity......................................78
Maximum capital gains tax rates......................................115
Maximum Tax Rate on Net Capital Gain............................145
Meals or lodging furnished 6
Medical expenses...79
Mid year convention 57
Miscellaneous Itemized Deductions..................................113
Mortgage Revenue Bond..46

N

Net Operating Loss (NOL)..187
No additional cost service, fringe benefit.............................9

Non-recourse liability..27

O

Ordinary and necessary expenses...66

P

Partner's distributive share..170
Partner, income and credits of 169
Partners, not partnership, is subject to tax.......................................169
Partnership computations..169
Passive activity losses..78
Pass-thru of items to C corporation shareholders 171
Pass-thru of items to S corporation shareholders.............................171
Personal Exemptions 120
Personal Exemptions, allowance for deductions...............................120
Personal Expenses..79
Personal services charitable deduction..97
Personal, living or family expense deduction 90
Phaseout, personal exemptions 121
Prepaid Subscription Income, accounting..180
Private Activity Bond..45
Private Activity Bond - 5% Test...45
Private business test 45
Private security test 45
Prizes and awards...24
Property Held in Trust..160
Property is acquired by gift rather then inherited 32
Property Transactions...125
Property transactions gain or loss realized and recognized 125
Property transactions, characterization of the gain or loss.................125
Property transferred in connection with performance of service 16
Property used in the trade or business...128
Property, realized gain...135
Property, realized loss, ...135

Q

Qualified 501 Bond...46
Qualified Bond..45
Qualified employee discount, fringe benefit 11
Qualified moving expenses fringe benefit..12
Qualified Pensions...199
Qualified transportation fringe...12

R

Realization on property 26
Recapture alimony payments...103
Recapture of depreciation 61
Recourse debt 27
Residence, sale - one time exclusion 142
Reversionary interest..165
Rollover of gain on sale of principal..139
Roth IRA 201

S

Salvage value 56
Savings And Loan, Losses from..198
Social Security benefits received..21
Special rule for gain on property transferred to trust at less than fair market
    value 162
Standard Deduction: 111
Start-up expenditures..53
Stepped-Up 31
Straight line method 56
Substantiate deductions - entertainment..85
Substantiation requirement - charitable contribution...........................96

T

Tax Benefit items, recovery of 191
Tax Benefit Rule..190
Tax consequences of divorce 98
Tax Credit...122
Tax exempt income - expenses...47
Tax imposed...161
Tax shelters..197
Tax Shelters, Conversion of ordinary income.....................................197
Tax Shelters, deferral of income 197
Taxable income...109
Taxable Income defined...111
Taxable income of the trust..162
Taxable income, Computation of 109
Taxable year 175
Taxation of Trusts..160
Threshold Amount, joint return..121
Throwback Rules 163
Trade or business expenses...66

Transfers of property between spouses incident to divorce......................106
Traveling Expenses...89
Trust income, deductions, and credits attributable to grantor trusts..........164
Trusts & Estates, inclusion of amounts in gross income of beneficiaries..163
Trusts distributing current income only, inclusion of amounts...............162

U

Unearned income..115
Using Deductions..118

V

Volume cap..46
Voluntariness..97

W

Wagering losses...38
Welfare payments received...21
Working condition fringe..11

Table of IRC § References

IRC § 1...3
IRC § 11...171
IRC § 21...123
IRC § 32...122
IRC § 55...205
IRC § 56...206
IRC § 57...206
IRC § 58...206
IRC § 61...10, 21, 22
IRC § 61(a)(1):..3, 13
IRC § 61(a)(3)...25
IRC § 61(a)(8)...98
IRC § 61(a)(12)...35
IRC § 62...110
IRC § 63...3, 111
IRC § 63(e)..112
IRC § 67...113
IRC § 68...113
IRC § 71...99
IRC § 72...34
IRC § 72(a)..34
IRC § 72(b)..34
IRC § 72(b)(3)(A)...34
IRC § 72(b)(3)(B)...35
IRC § 72(b)(3)(C)...34
IRC § 72(c)..35
IRC § 72(c)(3)(C)..35
IRC § 74...24
IRC § 79(a)..14
IRC § 83...16
IRC § 83(c)(1)..17
IRC § 83(c)(2)..17
IRC § 85...22
IRC § 86...21
IRC § 86(a)(2)..21
IRC § 101..15, 16
IRC § 101(a)(1)..15
IRC § 101(a)(1);...15
IRC § 101(a)(2)..15
IRC § 101(c)...16

IRC § 101(2)..29
IRC § 101(4)..29
IRC § 102...23
IRC § 102(a)..23
IRC § 102(b)..23
IRC § 102(c),...24
IRC § 103(a)..43
IRC § 103(b)..44
IRC § 104...40
IRC § 104(a)(2)...40
IRC § 104(a)(3))..42
IRC § 104(a)(3))..42
IRC § 104(a):...40
IRC § 105...42
IRC § 105(a)..42
IRC § 105(b)..42
IRC § 105(h)..43
IRC § 106...43
IRC § 107..7, 25
IRC § 108...35
IRC § 108(1)(3)...36
IRC § 108(a)(1)...36
IRC § 108(a)(1)(B)..36
IRC § 108(a)(1)(c)(g)...36
IRC § 108(a)(3))..36
IRC § 108(d)(1)(a),(b)...37
IRC § 108(d)(3))..36
IRC § 108(g)..36
IRC § 111..191
IRC § 117...24, 81, 82
IRC § 119..6
IRC § 119(a)...6
IRC § 119(a)(1)...13
IRC § 119(b)...6
IRC § 119(c)...7
IRC § 119(d)...7
IRC § 119(d)(2))..7
IRC § 121..141
IRC § 127...82
IRC § 132..8, 9
IRC § 132(1)..11
IRC § 132(j)(1)...9
IRC § 132(a)...8

IRC § 132(a)(2) 14
IRC § 132(b)...10
IRC § 132(b)(1) 9, 13
IRC § 132(c)...11
IRC § 132(d)..11
IRC § 132(e)..11
IRC § 132(e)(2) 12
IRC § 132(f) 12
IRC § 132(g)..12
IRC § 132(g)..12
IRC § 132(l) 9
IRC § 135 44
IRC § 141 45
IRC § 141(b)..45
IRC § 141(d)..46
IRC § 141(e)(1) 45
IRC § 143 46
IRC § 144 46
IRC § 145 46
IRC § 146 46
IRC § 148 47
IRC § 149 47
IRC § 151 ....3, 120
IRC § 152 ....3, 121
IRC § 162 ....6, 11, 39, 66
IRC § 162(c), (f) and (g),....................................39
IRC § 163 93
IRC § 163(d)...203
IRC § 164 94
IRC § 165 75
IRC § 165(d)..38
IRC § 165(g)...148
IRC § 167 ....11, 54
IRC § 168 55
IRC § 170 95
IRC § 172 187
IRC § 179 61
IRC § 183(b)...197
IRC § 195 53
IRC § 197 62
IRC § 212 72
IRC § 213 79
IRC § 215 99

IRC § 217 12
IRC § 263 49
IRC § 263A 51, 203
IRC § 263(c) 195
IRC § 265 47
IRC § 274(j) 25
IRC § 274(m) 6
IRC § 280A 72
IRC § 280E 39, 75
IRC § 401 199
IRC § 408 200
IRC § 441 175
IRC § 448 171
IRC § 453 180
IRC § 455 180
IRC § 456 181
IRC § 464 183
IRC § 465 203
IRC § 469 78
IRC § 471 184
IRC § 482 172
IRC § 501 173
IRC § 611 193
IRC § 612 193
IRC § 613 194
IRC § 641 161
IRC § 643 162
IRC § 644 162
IRC § 651 162
IRC § 661 163
IRC § 662 163
IRC § 671 164
IRC § 672 165
IRC § 673 165
IRC § 674 165
IRC § 675 166
IRC § 676 166
IRC § 678 166
IRC § 701 169
IRC § 702 169
IRC § 703 169
IRC § 704 170
IRC § 1001 ....25, 148

IRC § 1014 31
IRC § 1014(b)(9) 31
IRC § 1015 32
IRC § 1015(d)(6) 33
IRC § 1016 29
IRC § 1031 133
IRC § 1033 142
IRC § 1034 139
IRC § 1035 144
IRC § 1041 106
IRC § 1045 153
IRC § 1091 78
IRC § 1202 153
IRC § 1211 151
IRC § 1212 151
IRC § 1221 125
IRC § 1222 149
IRC § 1231 128
IRC § 1245 132
IRC § 1250 132
IRC § 1366 171